This book is sold in aid of Camphill Blair Drummond – a member of the international Camphill movement.

C.B.D., near Stirling in Scotland, provides further education, training in arts and crafts, and a wide variety of work experience for over 50 young adults with special needs.

HOME COOKING

A COLLECTION OF FAVOURITE RECIPES
FROM PARENTS AND FRIENDS OF
CAMPHILL BLAIR DRUMMOND

WYNSTONES PRESS

1st edition 1988.
Reprinted 1989.

Published on behalf of Camphill Blair Drummond by

Wynstones Press, Brookthorpe, Gloucester GL4 0UW. UK.

Printed by Wynstones Press.

British Library Cataloguing in Publication Data

Drummond, Camphill Blair
    Home cooking.
    I. Title
    641.5

ISBN 0-946206-10-4

Contents

Our bread is not our food;
What feeds us in the bread
Is God's eternal word,
His spirit and his life.

         Amen
by Angelus Silesius.

Acknowledgements

I am truly indebted to parents and friends, who so cheerfully parted with their favourite recipes. It is an honour to be able to include Her Majesty, the Queen Mother's recipe on page 135, which is only sold for charity. I am also especially grateful to the various celebrities who answered my request. The delightful illustrations and cover were done by David Newbatt, resident artist at Camphill Blair Drummond. Thanks must also go to Sally and Georg Schad and their Staff at C.B.D. for the festivals section.

Mairi Black.

Soups and Starters

Courgette and Carrot Soup *- or chilled vegetable juice*

4 ozs butter or margarine
1 lb carrots, pared and thinly sliced
1 lb courgettes, trimmed and thinly
  sliced
½ level tsp dried thyme
2 bay leaves

4 pints chicken stock
1 Tbsp tomato paste
4 ozs powder potatoes
Salt and pepper
Parsley

Melt butter in large pan. Add carrots and courgettes with thyme and bay leaves. Cover and saute for 10 minutes. Pour stock into pan, add tomato paste and stir, bringing to the boil. Cover and simmer for 30 minutes. Sieve or use electric blender, then return to the saucepan and add potato powder. Adjust seasoning. Serve garnished with fresh parsley. (Instead of using potato powder, use 1 lb potatoes with the carrots and courgettes.)

Audrey Cowan, Hamilton.

Quick Cream of Chicken Soup

2 ozs butter
1 medium onion, chopped
1½ Tbsps plain flour
1 small tin evaporated milk

3 chicken stock cubes dissolved in
  2 pints water
Salt and pepper
Chopped parsley

Cook chopped onion gently in the butter. Stir in flour and cook for 2 minutes; gradually stir in the hot milk and stock to make a smooth soup. Season to taste. Before serving sprinkle with chopped parsley.

Pat Scott, Edinburgh.

Vegetarian Cream of Cauliflower Soup

1 medium cauliflower
1 oz butter or margarine
1 pint white stock
Salt and pepper

½ oz cornflour
1 gill milk
1 egg yolk
1 Tbsp cream

Melt butter in pan. Divide the cauliflower into sprigs, tossing in the melted fat. Add the boiling stock and seasonings, then cover the pan and cook cauliflower until tender. Reserving a few small sprigs as garnish, sieve remainder of soup. Add cornflour with milk to the sieved soup and boil for 5 minutes stirring all the time. Allow to cool. Strain in yolk and cream and cook until yolk thickens soup. Add garnish of sprigs to soup and serve.

Jean Simpson, Grangemouth.

Cauliflower Soup

1 medium cauliflower	1 blade mace
1 onion, sliced	Salt and pepper
2 or 3 bacon rinds	½ oz flour
½ or 1 oz butter	¼ pint milk
1½ pints stock	A little chopped parsley

Boil cauliflower for a few minutes. Drain and cut into pieces. Take sliced onion and saute in the bacon rind fat, then add the cauliflower and a little butter if necessary. Pour on the stock and add mace and seasonings. Simmer for ¾ hour until tender. Blend soup, having removed mace, and stir in flour blended with milk. Bring to boil and cook for 2 or 3 minutes. Add chopped parsley.

Wilma Aitken, Aberdeen.

Cream of Carrot Soup

1½ lbs carrots, sliced	2 tsps tomato purée or paste
1½ pints chicken stock	6 fl ozs single cream
2 tsps salt	½ tsp pepper
2 Tbsps butter	1 Tbsp parsley
1 Tbsp plain flour	

Put carrots in saucepan and add enough stock to cover. Add 1 tsp salt and bring to boil, then simmer until soft purée. Melt butter over moderate heat. Remove from heat, stir in flour and mix to a smooth paste. Return saucepan to heat and gradually stir in about ⅓ of remaining stock and then the carrot purée. Add remainder of stock, stirring to mix well and bring mixture to boil. Remove from heat and stir in tomato paste and cream. Return to low heat to warm, adding pepper and parsley.

Mrs. E. Ormiston, Inverary.

Chilled Fordell Cherry Soup

12 ozs fresh black cherries
    or 2 x 15 oz tins, well drained
½ pint red table wine

¼ pint fresh orange juice
1 Tbsp caster sugar
2 Tbsps brandy

Stone cherries and put in a pan with the red wine, orange juice and sugar. Bring to the boil and simmer for 5 minutes. Remove 2 Tbsps of cherries and set aside. Blend remaining cherries with cooking liquid in liquidiser until smooth. Add brandy and chill overnight. Add remaining cherries before serving.

Nicholas Fairbairn Q.C., M.P.

Carrot and Orange Soup

1 oz butter
1 clove garlic, crushed
1 medium onion, chopped
1 lb carrots, coarsely grated
1½ pints water
2 Tbsps orange juice
Finely grated zest of 1 orange
1 tsp tomato purée
1 chicken stock cube

Salt and freshly ground black
    pepper
2 Tbsps cold water
1 tsp cornflour, omit if using cream
¼ pint single cream
Dash of sherry
Orange slices
1 tsp parsley

Melt the butter in a saucepan. Add the crushed garlic, chopped onion and grated carrots. Stir and cover for 5 minutes over a low heat. Add the water, orange juice and zest, tomato puree and stock cube. Season to taste, cover and simmer for 30 minutes. Mix the cornflour, if used, with cold water. Stir into the soup and simmer for another 5 minutes. Liquidise. Stir in the cream and sherry, heat without boiling. Garnish with orange slices and parsley.

Pat Scott, Edinburgh.

Corn Chowder

2 ozs butter
3 onions, peeled and sliced
3 potatoes, peeled and sliced
¾ pint milk

11½ ozs creamed sweet corn
2 tsps parsley
Seasoning

Melt butter, add onions and potatoes, then cook gently for 10 minutes. Stir in the milk, sweetcorn, parsley and seasoning. Cover and simmer for 20 minutes until soft. A good tasty soup.

Muriel Gilray, Edinburgh.

A Gentle Soup for a Tender Stomach

Flour or semolina
Cooking oil or butter

Caraway seeds
Salt

A cupful of flour or semolina is added to some hot oil or butter in a frying pan. Add a good pinch of caraway seeds and salt. Stir mixture with a wooden spoon until flour is brown. Then carefully add water and let mixture boil for some minutes. Stir well adding more water when necessary.

Georg Schad, Camphill Blair Drummond.

Fish and Lemon Soup

1½ lbs cod or haddock
Juice of 1 lemon
Sea salt and black pepper
8 ozs carrots
1 oz butter
2 medium onions, thinly sliced
1 medium cucumber, thinly sliced

8 ozs tomatoes, chopped
10 black olives, halved and stoned
2 pints fish stock
1 Tbsp thyme
2 Tbsps parsley
4 slices lemon

Cut fish into strips, sprinkle on lemon juice, salt and pepper and leave for 2 hours. Cut carrots thinly or in sticks. Melt butter and stir in the onions and carrots, then cook until soft. Stir in the cucumber and cook for 2 minutes. Add tomatoes and cook until they are reduced to a purée.

Mrs E. Ormiston, Inverary.

Lettuce Soup

¾ oz butter
2 onions, chopped roughly
4 potatoes, peeled and diced

2 pints good stock
1 lettuce, washed and separated
Cream to garnish

Melt butter in soup pot and gently toss onions and potatoes for 5 minutes. Add stock and lettuce and boil for 45 minutes. Cool slightly and liquidise. Serve garnished with cream.

Sadie MacQueen, Balvicar.

Scotch Broth

1 Tbsp butter
1 carrot, chopped
1 turnip, chopped
1 leek, chopped

1½ pints mutton stock
1½ ozs pearl barley
Salt and pepper
1 tsp chopped parsley

Melt butter in a soup pan. Add chopped vegetables and toss over a low heat. Add stock, barley and seasonings. Simmer gently for 30 - 45 minutes. Serve with chopped parsley.

Pat Scott, Edinburgh.

Beetroot and Red Cabbage Soup

2 Tbsps oil
1 medium onion, peeled and
  chopped
12 ozs red cabbage, shredded
1 tsp dried dill
¼ tsp caraway seeds
1 bay leaf

3 medium beetroots, peeled and
  grated
1½ Tbsps lemon juice
1¼ pints water or vegetable cube
  stock
Sea salt and black pepper
Chopped parsley and yogurt

Saute onion and cabbage for 5 minutes in oil. Add dill, caraway seeds and bay leaf. Stir in beetroot, lemon juice and stock. Bring to boil and simmer for 15 minutes. Serve with chopped parsley and a little yogurt on top.

Jean Inglis, Edinburgh.

Onion Soup

1 medium onion, peeled and
  chopped
2 ozs butter

1½ pints stock (2 stock cubes)
Salt and pepper
1 small tin evaporated milk

Melt the butter in pan and cook onion until soft but not coloured, then gradually add the stock, stirring all the time. Cook for 10 minutes. Add the tin of evaporated milk before serving.

Jean Simpson, Grangemouth.

Cream of Tomato Soup

Knob of butter
5 medium potatoes, thinly sliced
1 medium onion, thinly sliced
4 pints hot water

Salt, pepper and sugar
Chicken cube
15 oz tin of tomatoes
2 Tbsps top of milk, or cream

Melt butter in soup pot and fry onion and potatoes until fat disappears – do NOT brown. Add hot water with tomatoes, salt and pepper to taste, plus ½ tsp sugar and chicken cube. Bring to the boil. Simmer for 30 minutes. Liquidise then return to pot, add top of milk. Heat up but don't boil.
For an **Asparagus** or **Celery** soup, make as above, but omit sugar. Also, after liquidising, sieve soup before adding cream.

Mairi Black, Rutherglen.

Cocky-Leeky Soup

1 boiling fowl
6 leeks, chopped
1 large grated carrot

2 ozs rice
Salt and pepper
1 Tbsp chopped parsley

Simmer the fowl in 6 pints of water for 2–3 hours. Allow to cool. Skim well. The white meat of the fowl can be used in other dishes and the brown meat chopped up and added to the stock with the leeks, carrot, rice and seasonings. Simmer for 30 minutes then add parsley just before serving.

Pat Scott, Edinburgh.

Meatball Soup - a meal on its own

4 cups diced potato
1 tsp mixed or allspice
Chopped parsley
Salt and pepper
2 carrots, sliced
4 cups water

For the meatballs:
1 lb mince
1 cup breadcrumbs
1 cup milk
1 tsp salt

Make small meatballs by mixing ingredients together. Mix all remaining ingredients and bring to boil, then add the meatballs. Cook slowly for 30 minutes or 6 minutes in pressure cooker. Add 1 cup of milk or cream and 4 tsp vinegar. Thicken and add peas and any other vegetables if desired.

Sarah Scott, Broughty Ferry.

Griesklösschen Suppe - Soup with Semolina Dumplings

1 litre soup stock (vegetable or meat)

For the dumplings:
1½ ozs butter
3 ozs semolina

1 egg
Salt, nutmeg and parsley

Beat the butter until soft. Add semolina slowly and whisk the egg in. Season with salt, nutmeg and parsley. Form small dumplings with a teaspoon and put them in the boiling stock. Let them boil for 20 minutes and then lower the heat for another 5 minutes.

Renate Seubert (Germany), Camphill Blair Drummond.

Spinach Soup

1 lb fresh spinach
A few outer lettuce leaves
1 small onion, chopped
1 pint chicken stock

Salt and pepper
1 oz butter
1 Tbsp flour
½ pint milk

1 oz butter   Cream or plain yogurt
1 tsp lemon juice

Wash spinach and lettuce and chop finely (can be done in food processor).
Soften onion gently in the butter, then add spinach and lettuce. Cook for a
few minutes, stirring occasionally. Add stock, lemon juice and seasoning.
Simmer for not more than 10 minutes. Cool and sieve, or liquidise. Make
white sauce with butter, flour and milk, then gradually add liquidised
mixture. Adjust seasoning if necessary.
This soup should remain a pale green colour and can either be served hot or
cold. The addition of a swirl of cream or yogurt improves its appearance.

Maggie Sherriff, Blair Drummond.

Cream of Watercress Soup

1 medium onion, chopped   ½ pint milk
1 small potato, chopped   ½ pint vegetable stock
Knob butter   Salt and pepper to taste
Bunch watercress   4 Tbsps fresh double cream

Melt butter in saucepan and saute onion until transparent. Add potato,
watercress, milk and stock. Bring to the boil, then cover and simmer for 20
minutes. Allow to cool slightly, then blend small amounts in liquidiser.
Return to pan, adjust seasoning, stir in cream and reheat to serving
temperature. Can be served either hot or cold.

Jean Inglis, Edinburgh.

Jellied Florida Cocktail - *serves 4*

1 tin grapefruit   1 lemon table jelly
1 tin mandarin oranges   4 cherries

Use the juice of grapefruit and oranges to make up the lemon jelly. Arrange
grapefruit and oranges in four glasses. Pour over slightly cooled jelly. Serve
chilled with a cherry on top.

Nancy Clelland, Blackwood.

Hot Citrus with Port

2 large tins unsweetened grapefruit
  segments
2 large tins mandarin oranges

1 large tin orange segments
1 cup of port

Drain all the fruit and place in a saucepan with just less than a cupful of the juice. Heat slowly. Put into glasses and pour hot port over each. Serve immediately.

P. M. Oldfield, Middlesborough.

Cold Kebab Starter *- serves 4*

1 Avocado
1 Grapefruit
½ small melon
1 small yellow pepper
1 small red pepper

For the sauce:
2 Tbsps fresh orange juice
2 Tbsps golden syrup
½ level tsp ginger

Wash and prepare the 5 basic ingredients and cut into pieces about 1 inch square. Thread onto 4 skewers.
Prepare sauce by mixing ingredients together thoroughly. Put sauce into 4 individual dishes.

Audrey Cowan, Hamilton

Mixed Fruit Cocktail

1 measure cucumber
1 measure melon
1 measure avocado
1 measure tomato, de-seeded and
  skinned

Salt and pepper
1 Tbsp mixed herbs
French dressing
Sugar

Cut all ingredients into approximately equal sized chunks or cubes. Place fruits in a bowl, season and sprinkle with mixed herbs. Dress liberally with basic French dressing, with a little sugar. Chill well.

P. M. Oldfield, Middlesborough.

Nutty Peaches - *serves 2*

4 peach halves
4 lettuce leaves
3 ozs sweetcorn
1 oz salted peanuts
4 ozs Cheddar cheese, grated

1 – 2 Tbsps whipped cream
1 – 2 Tbsps salad cream
Seasoning
4 slices cucumber

Drain the peach halves and place each on a lettuce leaf. Mix the sweetcorn, nuts and cheese, and bind together with the whipped cream and salad cream. Season to taste. Pile mixture on the top of each peach. Garnish with cucumber.

Mairi Black, Rutherglen.

Smoked Mackerel Paté

2 large smoked mackerels
5 oz carton of sour cream
1 hard boiled egg

1 garlic clove, crushed
Salt and pepper
Juice of about ½ lemon

Skin mackerel. Liquidise all ingredients and refrigerate. Serve with toast.

Averill Marks, St. Andrews.

Quick Tuna Paté

1 large tin tuna, drained
2 ozs butter
1 tsp lemon juice
1 – 2 Tbsps double cream

2 heaped Tbsps fresh parsley
Salt and freshly ground black
    pepper

Place all ingredients into a either a liquidiser or blender and process for about 30 – 40 seconds, until well blended. Serve with Melba Toast

P. M. Oldfield, Middlesborough.

Plockrapool Prawns *- starter or tea time course*

1 lb frozen prawns
4 eggs, hard boiled and chopped

4 ozs parsley, chopped finely
Ingredients for cheese sauce

Make a good cheese sauce, using Scotch Cheddar. Season with salt and plenty of black pepper. Add the prawns, eggs and parsley. Serve hot with wholemeal bread or rolls. Suggest serving in small bowls.

Moira Cousins, Glasgow.

Seafood Chowder

½ - ¾ pint thick white sauce
1 jar mussels

1 jar of cockles
1 tin of shrimps or prawns

Drain the shellfish then fold into white sauce and put either into ramekin dishes or onto scallop shells. Sprinkle a little cheese on top of each and grill for a few minutes. These can be made the day before and heated in the oven. Recommended to serve with brown bread and butter.

P. M. Oldfield, Middlesborough.

Marinated Kipper Fillets *- a delicious starter for a dinner party or light lunch*

1 lb kipper fillets, fresh or frozen
1 small onion
A few bay leaves, fresh if possible

For Marinade:
3 Tbsps wine vinegar
4 Tbsps olive or sunflower oil
1 level tsp caster sugar
Salt and freshly ground black
   pepper

Remove skin from kipper fillets and arrange in pieces in a serving dish with onion rings and bay leaves. Combine ingredients for marinade by shaking together in a screw-top jar and pour over the kippers. Leave overnight in fridge, or for several hours, to allow marinade to be absorbed. Serve with slices of brown bread for a starter, or with a salad for a light lunch.

Anne Carter, St. Andrews.

Tuna Mousse - *serves 4*

6½ oz can tuna, drained
2 beaten eggs
½ pint milk
4 ozs Cheddar cheese, grated
4 Tbsps mayonnaise

1 stick celery, finely chopped
Salt and pepper
Lemon wedges
Parsley

Oven temperature: 310°F. 155°C. Gas mark 2.

Preheat oven. Mash tuna in a bowl, then add the eggs, milk, cheese, mayonnaise, celery, salt and pepper. Mix thoroughly. Place mixture into 4 buttered ovenproof dishes. Smooth tops. Bake for approximately 40 minutes. Serve hot with lemon wedges, parsley and fingers of hot toast. May be served cold if desired.

Staff, Eastern General Hospital, Edinburgh.

Prawn Starter

Large packet frozen prawns,
  defrosted and water gently
  squeezed out
3 eggs, hard boiled then coarsely
  chopped
4 large tomatoes, skinned,
  de-seeded and coarsely chopped
5 ozs Cheddar cheese, grated
1 cupful of fresh breadcrumbs

For the Bechamel sauce:
Knob of butter
½ oz flour
½ pint milk
Seasonings

Oven temperature: 350°F. 175°C. Gas mark 4.

Make the Bechamel sauce and add 4 ozs of the grated cheese, making sure the sauce is not too runny. Mix the prawns, eggs and tomatoes together and put into a shallow dish. Gently stir in the cheese sauce. Sprinkle breadcrumbs, mixed with the remaining cheese over the top. Bake in a moderate oven until crumbs on top are crisp. Serve with toast. This can also be used as a supper dish, served with a green salad.

Grapefruit, Apple and Salmon Salad

1 tin grapefruit
2 dessert apples, chopped

1 small tin salmon
French dressing or wine vinegar

Drain and flake the salmon. Arrange grapefruit, chopped apples and salmon in 4 glasses. Pour over a little French dressing or wine vinegar. Serve chilled.

Nancy Clelland, Blackwood.

Lentil Paté - *serves 6*

9 ozs split red lentils
1 – 1½ pints chicken stock
1 onion finely chopped
4½ tsps tomato puree
2 tsps dried mixed herbs

Salt and freshly ground black
 pepper
2 ozs curd cheese
Coriander sprig to garnish

Put lentils in a large saucepan. Pour in stock, add onion, tomato purée and herbs. Season to taste. Bring to boil, lower heat and simmer for 30 minutes, stirring frequently until lentils are swollen and stock absorbed. Remove from heat and leave to cool – about 30 minutes. Transfer lentil mixture to a blender and work until smooth, then add the curd cheese, a piece at a time. Taste pate and adjust seasoning if necessary. Spoon mixture into a 1½ pint serving dish. Level the surface and leave until cold. Cover the paté and refrigerate for 2 hours before serving. Garnish with coriander and serve straight from the dish. Suggest serving with toasted granary bread.

Rhoda Burdis, Brampton.

Farmhouse Roll - *a kind of English Country Paté*

¼ pint milk
3 – 4 slices wholemeal bread
¾ lb rump steak
½ lb gammon
1 medium onion
2 – 3 sprigs parsley

2 level tsps salt
Freshly ground black pepper
½ lb pork sausagemeat
1 egg lightly mixed
2 hard boiled eggs, optional
Browned breadcrumbs

Heat milk in a saucepan. Remove from heat and break bread slices into milk and leave to soak for 10 minutes, then blend until smooth. Trim excess fat from steak and rind from the gammon. Cut onion into quarters and mince with the steak, gammon and parsley, first through a coarse and then a fine blade. Add the blended milk, bread and seasoning. Press the mixture into a greased 2 lb stone jar or basin, pressing the hard boiled eggs into the centre. Cover with a double layer of greaseproof paper, tie down and cover with a square of kitchen foil. Half fill a deep saucepan with hot water. Bring to the boil then stand the jar in the water. Cover with lid and simmer for 2½ – 3 hours. When cooked, remove paper, cover with fresh greaseproof paper and top with saucer and a heavy weight. Stand overnight until cold. To remove from jar, dip in hot water for a moment, then shake onto a square of paper.

Anne Carter, St. Andrews.

Stuffed Mushrooms

1 cup uniform size mushrooms
Croutons of fried bread
Paprika pepper

For stuffing:
3 Tbsps cooked and chopped bacon
or ham, optional
2 tsps chopped parsley
2 Tbsps cooked and chopped onion
1 Tbsp white sauce

Oven temperature: 330°F. 165°C. Gas Mark 3.

Remove stalks from mushrooms and place on a well greased baking tray. Mix together ingredients for stuffing and place in mushrooms. Cover with well greased paper. Bake for 10 – 15 minutes. Place on croutons of fried bread and dust with paprika. Stuffed mushrooms can be used as a course on their own or as a garnish for other dishes.

Pat Scott, Edinburgh.

FISH

Bonne Femme: Fish and Mushrooms

1 onion, skinned and chopped
2 tsps flour
4 ozs minced mushrooms
4 fillets white fish

¾ cup water
1½ Tbsps lemon juice
1 tsp parsley

Mix all ingredients together and cook in a frying pan, covering with lid.

Lockhart McEwan, Rutherglen.

South African Pickled Fish *- serves 6 - 8 as a main course, or 12 as part of a buffet*

2¼ lbs haddock fillet
4 ozs seasoned flour

2 eggs, beaten
Oil for shallow frying

For curry sauce:
¾ pint light malt vinegar
⅓ pint water
3 Tbsps brown sugar
3 tsps hot or mild curry powder
1½ tsps ground turmeric

1 tsp plain flour
8 bay leaves
½ tsp salt
20 peppercorns
3 – 4 large onions, peeled and sliced

Garnish with red and green peppers and lemon

Cook at least 2 days in advance.

Cut fish into eight 3 x 2 inch pieces. Dip first in flour, then in egg, then back in flour. Fry until cooked and golden.

For the sauce, pour the vinegar, water and sugar in a saucepan. Stir over a low heat until sugar dissolves. Blend 1 Tbsp of this liquid with curry powder, turmeric and flour. Away from heat, stir the paste into the pan, then add bay leaves, salt and peppercorns. Bring to boil, stirring constantly, then add onion slices. Cook for 5 minutes and then cool.

Place a layer of fish in a large casserole and cover with some onion. Repeat in layers until all the fish and onions are used. Pour over the sauce. Cover with lid and leave in a cool place for at least 2 days. Garnish with fresh bay leaves, red and green pepper and lemon slices. Serve with a rice salad, grated carrot, chutney and desiccated coconut.

Staff, Eastern General Hospital, Edinburgh.

Thela's Chinese Style Fish

4 haddock fillets
4 ozs S.R. flour
Pinch of salt

1 egg
¼ pint water

For Pineapple sauce:
1 small tin pineapple pieces
1 Tbsp soft brown sugar
1 Tbsp cornflour
2 Tbsps vinegar
1 Tbsp soy sauce

1 tsp finely grated or chopped
  ginger
¼ pint syrup from pineapple
Salt to taste
Oil for deep frying

Cut haddock into bite sized pieces. Make a batter mixing the flour and salt, adding the egg and water gradually. Beat until smooth. Add the fish pieces and deep fry until golden brown. Keep warm.

For the pineapple sauce, mix the following in a pan: brown sugar, cornflour, vinegar, soy sauce, ginger, pineapple syrup. Bring to the boil and simmer for 2 – 3 minutes, then add the pineapple pieces and reheat sauce. Pour the sauce over the fish pieces and serve with rice.

Moira Cousins, Glasgow.

Smoked Haddock with Crunchy Topping

4 smoked fillets
½ pint single or double cream

2 tomatoes
1 tsp mixed herbs

For the topping:
3 ozs plain flour
2 ozs margarine

2 ozs cheese

Oven temperature: 370°F. 190°C. Gas mark 5.

Arrange the fish in a dish with the cream, herbs and tomatoes. Rub flour into fat, add grated cheese and sprinkle on top of fish. Bake for 40 minutes.

Eileen Dunn, Rutherglen.

Haddock Pie

½ lb filleted haddock, cooked and flaked
1 small cup of breadcrumbs

2 eggs, separated
Salt and pepper
Milk

Mix the fish and breadcrumbs. Add the egg yolks and seasoning. Add enough milk to mix to a soft consistency. Beat egg whites until stiff then fold into mixture. Turn into a greased bowl, cover with greased paper and steam for about 40 minutes. Serve with a cheese sauce.

Mairi Black, Rutherglen.

Stuffed Whiting Roll with Bacon

3 – 4 tail end fillets of whiting
4 ozs grated cheese
1 small onion, skinned and chopped
3 – 4 slices of bacon
Salt and pepper

Margarine
4 skewers or cocktail sticks
Parsley and grilled tomatoes for decoration

Oven temperature: 350°F. 175°C. Gas mark 4.

Cut the fillets in half – lengthwise – and remove the skin. Mix the cheese, onions and seasoning, then spread onto whiting. Close ½ fillets together with filling in centre and wrap bacon around each fillet. Secure with skewer or cocktail stick. Put into casserole and dot fish with margarine. Bake for 25 – 30 minutes in a moderate oven until golden brown. Decorate with parsley and grilled tomatoes.

Mairi Black, Rutherglen.

Hot or Cold Thrifty Salmon

1 small tin pink salmon
2 eggs, beaten
1 tsp Worcester sauce

1 cup fresh white breadcrumbs
Salt and pepper

Mash the salmon very well with a fork. Mix eggs well with salmon, sauce, breadcrumbs, salt and pepper. Turn into a buttered bowl. Cover and steam for 1 hour. Serve hot or cold.

Kathleen Montgomery, Aberdeen.

Salmon Steaks in Edinburgh Sauce

6 salmon steaks
Cayenne pepper
Salt and pepper
2 Tbsps flour

2 Tbsps anchovy essence, may be
   omitted
2 glasses dry sherry
¾ pint double cream

Oven temperature: 330°F. 165°C. Gas mark 3.

Thoroughly grease a shallow ovenproof dish. Mix together the Cayenne pepper, salt, pepper and flour, and dust over the salmon. Arrange in the dish and pour the other ingredients over. Bake for 30 minutes. Serve either hot or cold. May be garnished with stuffed mushrooms or parsley.

Pat Scott, Edinburgh.

Salmon Mousse

7 oz tin pink salmon
4 ozs Hellman's mayonnaise
4 ozs fresh cream

1 tsp lemon juice
1 sachet gelatine

Remove the skin and bones from the salmon, place in a bowl and mix thoroughly. Add the mayonnaise and cream, then mix with a whisk. Add the lemon juice. Mix gelatine in boiling water and add to the mixture, stirring well. Leave in the fridge for 30 minutes.

Miss Lynch, Eastern General Hospital, Edinburgh.

Trout in Sour Cream Sauce

6 trout, gutted and cleaned
3 ozs seasoned flour
4 ozs butter

½ tsp salt
¼ tsp black pepper
1 tsp paprika

2 Tbsps oil
12 ozs small mushrooms

1 tsp lemon juice
½ pint sour cream

Coat the fish with flour. Melt half the butter in a frying pan. Add the fish and fry for 5 minutes on each side, or until browned and cooked. Remove and keep hot. Pour off and discard the juices from pan. Place remaining butter and oil in the pan and stir in any sediment. Add the mushrooms and cook for 5 minutes. Add salt, pepper, paprika, lemon juice and sour cream. Stir constantly. Cook for 2 – 3 minutes but do not boil. Pour over fish and serve.

Mrs. E. Ormiston, Inverary.

Tuna Casserole

1 large tin tuna
1 small tin sweetcorn
1 small tin pineapple pieces
2 ozs chopped almonds
2 ozs grated cheese

½ pint white sauce
Salt, pepper, curry powder and
  mixed herbs to taste
1 tsp piquant jam or jelly
Crushed flakes, corn or bran

Oven temperature: 370°F. 190°C. Gas mark 5.

Make the white sauce. Add flaked fish, sweetcorn, drained pineapple, almonds, cheese and all the seasonings. Place in a greased casserole and top with crushed flakes, corn or bran – mixed with extra cheese. Bake in oven for 25 – 30 minutes.

Jean Inglis, Edinburgh.

Tuna Crisps Casserole

1 small tin tuna
1 tin condensed mushroom or
  celery soup

4 ozs milk
1 Tbsp Worcester sauce
1 cup crushed potato crisps

Oven temperature: 350°F. 175°C. Gas mark 4.

Flake tuna fish and mix with the undiluted soup, milk and Worcester sauce. Turn into a greased casserole dish. Sprinkle with crisps. Bake in a moderate oven for about 25 minutes.

Kathleen Montgomery, Aberdeen.

Tuna Fish Cannelloni

16 large cannelloni tubes
1 medium tin tuna fish
1 onion, chopped
1 cup brown bread crumbs
1 small egg
1 tsp mixed herbs
1 tsp oregano

For sauce:
2 tins tomatoes
Salt and black pepper
1 tsp mixed herbs

Oven temperature: 350°F. 175°C. Gas mark 4.

Make the sauce by beating together all the ingredients. Line an ovenproof dish with ½ inch of sauce. Mix together the tuna, onion, breadcrumbs, egg and herbs. Stuff cannelloni with mixture – not too tightly – and line up in dish, not touching each other. Cover with remainder of sauce. Bake in a moderate oven for 45 minutes or until the pasta is soft.

Lisa Starrs, Edinburgh.

Cheese and Tuna Pizza

For the base:
6 ozs cooked, sieved potatoes
6 ozs S.R. flour
1 tsp baking powder
1 tsp salt
1 tsp mixed herbs
2 Tbsps cooking oil
2 Tbsps water

For the topping:
10½ oz can condensed chicken
   soup
7 ozs flaked tuna
½ Tbsp chopped onion
2 ozs rolled oats
4 ozs grated cheese
½ tsp oregano

Oven temperature: 430°F. 220°C. Gas mark 7.

Mix together all the ingredients for the base and knead for 1 – 2 minutes to a soft dough. Place on a greased baking tray. Mix together the soup, tuna and onion, and spread on top of the base. Mix together remaining ingredients and sprinkle on top. Bake for about 20 minutes until golden brown.

Sarah Scott, Broughty Ferry.

Egg and Tuna Chowder

2 large tins tuna
4 eggs, hard boiled

1 pint thick white sauce
Grated cheese

Break tuna into chunks and halve peeled eggs. Place eggs flat side down in a dish alternatively with the tuna. Pour over white sauce and sprinkle with cheese and warm in oven for about 15 minutes.

P. M. Oldfield, Middlesborough.

Tasty Tuna Fish Cakes

1 small tin tuna
1 lb cold mashed potatoes
Chopped parsley

Salt and pepper
Fat for frying

Empty fish into a basin after draining off the oil. Mix with mashed potato, parsley, salt and pepper. Shape into round cakes, flour and fry in a little hot fat for a few minutes on each side.

Kathleen Montgomery, Aberdeen.

Tuna Kedgeree - *serves 4*

5 ozs long grain brown rice
Salt
3 hard boiled eggs
8 ozs natural yogurt
2 tsps curry powder

Freshly ground black pepper
2 x 7 oz tins tuna, drained and
  flaked
Sweet paprika to garnish

Cook the rice in plenty of salted boiling water until tender; drain and rinse well. Place in a warmed, oiled, shallow serving dish, cover and keep warm in a low oven. Chop 1 hard boiled egg and the white of the others, reserving the yolks. Warm yogurt in a small saucepan over a low heat – do not boil. Stir in the curry powder and pepper to taste, then beat until smooth with a wooden spoon. Fold in the tuna and chopped egg and warm through. Pour this sauce over the rice and fork it lightly. Press the reserved egg yolks through a sieve over the top of the kedgeree. Sprinkle with paprika to taste. Serve at once.

Suggested serving: Accompany with a green salad and mango chutney or ½ cucumber, thinly sliced and dressed with 5 ozs natural yogurt.

Rhoda Burdis, Brampton.

Soused Herring

4 fresh herrings	¼ tsp salt
1 piece mace	1 bay leaf
6 peppercorns	2 cloves
¼ pint vinegar	¼ pint water
1 chopped onion, optional	

Oven temperature: 350°F. 175°C. Gas mark 4.

Clean and bone the herrings. Roll up tightly from tail end. Place in a pie dish with all the ingredients. Bake in a moderate oven for 20 – 35 minutes. Allow to cool in liquor and serve with salad.

Pat Scott, Edinburgh.

Stegt Sild med Løgsovs - *Fried Herrings and Onion Sauce*

8 medium sized herrings	*For the onion sauce:*
2 eggs, beaten	2 Tbsps butter
Breadcrumbs	2 Tbsps flour
2 Tbsps flour	1 pint milk
	3 large onions, finely chopped
	Salt and sugar to taste

Rinse and bone the herrings. Dip in 2 Tbsps of flour, then the beaten eggs and thereafter the breadcrumbs. Fry in plenty of butter.
To make the sauce, melt butter in a pot over a low heat. Stir in flour and add milk, keeping the mixture smooth. Cook until thickened. Add the onions and bring to the boil. Onions may be boiled first in a little water. Season with salt and sugar. Serve with boiled potatoes.

Henrietta Nicolaisen, Denmark.

MEAT AND POULTRY

To "Love and Honour" are O.K.
And one might promise to obey,
But what makes wives turn slowly grey
Is what to cook each blessed day.

Meat Shape

1 lb lean smoked ham
1 lb lean stewing steak
6 oz breadcrumbs
1 tsp salt

1 tsp pepper
¼ tsp of ground mace and grated
   nutmeg
1 large egg

Remove skin from ham. Put ham and steak through a mincer or food processor. Add all the remaining ingredients, work them all together and steam for 3 hours in a meat mould. Leave in mould until cold.

Jean Inglis, Edinburgh.

Potted Hough

1 knap bone
1 lb hough

4 pints cold water
Seasoning

Boil bone for 2 hours and then strain. Put meat into stock and boil for 3 hours more. Stir well. Take meat out of pot and chop finely. Mix meat and stock, then turn into small dishes and leave to set.

Ena Barrie, Motherwell.

Dutch Roast

½ – ¾ lb mince
1 small onion, finely chopped
1 teacup breadcrumbs

1½ teacups milk
Salt and pepper

Oven temperature: 370°F. 190°C. Gas mark 5.

Preheat oven. Grease loaf tin or pie-dish. Soak breadcrumbs in milk. Rinse mince, mix with onion, breadcrumbs and milk. Season. Mix together with a fork until the mince is broken up. Put firmly into a loaf tin. Bake for ¾ – 1 hour.

Mairi Black, Rutherglen.

Bitokes a la Russe - *Hamburgers with cream sauce*

1½ lbs lean minced beef
3 ozs finely chopped onions
1 oz softened butter, ground beef
   suet or fresh pork fat
1½ tsps salt
Pinch of pepper
Pinch of thyme
1 egg

For the sauce:
2½ fl ozs stock or beef bouillon
¼ pint cream
Salt and pepper
Pinch of nutmeg
Lemon juice
1 – 1½ ozs softened butter
2 Tbsps chopped green herbs, such
   as parsley, chives, tarragon,
   chervil, *or* parsley only.

Add the beef, butter or fat, seasonings and egg to the onions in a mixing bowl and beat vigorously to blend thoroughly. Correct seasoning. Form into patties ¾ inch thick. Take ½ oz butter and ½ Tbsp oil, or enough to fill the bottom of a frying pan. Cook over moderate heat. Remove to hot serving dish.

To make the sauce, pour the fat out of the frying pan. Add the stock or bouillon and boil it down rapidly, scraping up coagulates of cooking juices until reduced almost to a syrup. Pour in cream and boil it down rapidly for a minute or two until it has been reduced and thickened slightly. Season to taste with salt, pepper, nutmeg and drops of lemon juice. Finally, removing the frying pan from the heat, swirl in the butter by spoon until it is absorbed. Stir in the chopped green herbs, spoon the sauce over the hamburgers and serve.

Ronnie Corbett, T.V. Celebrity.

Canadian Quickies

8 ozs cooked minced beef
1 onion, minced
2 ozs flour

1 oz suet, shredded
1 egg
Salt and pepper

Oven temperature: 350°F. 175°C. Gas mark 4.

Mix the meat, onion, flour and suet together in a bowl. Season well. Beat the egg and bind the mixture with it. Using a Tbsp, place rounds of the mixture into a greased baking tin. Bake in a moderate oven for about 30 minutes until cooked through and crisp.
Serve with new or creamed potatoes and gravy.

Kathleen Montgomery, Aberdeen.

Marzetti

1 lb mince	10 oz tin condensed tomato soup
1 large onion, chopped	Seasoning
10 oz tin condensed mushroom	½ lb red cheese, grated
soup	5 ozs egg noodles

Oven temperature: 350°F. 175°C. Gas mark 4.

Brown the mince and add the chopped onion. Add soup and mix well. Add seasoning and grated cheese. Cook noodles quickly for 5 minutes in boiling water, drain — not too thoroughly — and add to mixture. Put in casserole, cover and cook for 1¼ hours.

Eileen Dunn, Rutherglen.

Beef and Rice Casserole - *serves 6*

2 Tbsps cooking oil	1¼ cups boiling water
1 lb minced beef	½ cup uncooked long grain rice
½ cup chopped green pepper	1 tsp salt
⅓ cup chopped onion	¼ tsp pepper
½ cup sliced mushrooms	½ cup of flaked almonds
1 cup chopped celery	2 Tbsps melted butter
10 oz tin chicken and rice soup	

Oven temperature: 370°F. 190°C. Gas mark 5.

Heat oil in a heavy frying pan. Add beef and cook until lightly browned, stirring well. Add pepper, onion, mushrooms and celery, then cook gently until tender.

Put soup and water into a large saucepan and bring to the boil quickly. Reduce heat, add rice and stir. Cover and simmer for 20 minutes, by which time the rice will be tender and the liquid nearly all absorbed. Stir into this the mince and seasonings, then pour into a casserole dish. Sprinkle with almonds and drizzle butter over top. Bake for 20 minutes.

Pat Scott, Edinburgh.

Italienne Macaroni

2 onions	1 aubergine
1 lb mince	1 courgette
White sauce	1 tin tomatoes
½ lb mushrooms	Seasoning, garlic and mixed herbs
2 tomatoes	Pasta shells
1 green pepper	½ lb cheese, grated
1 red pepper	

Fry onions until lightly brown. Brown mince and add white sauce. Lightly fry mushrooms, tomatoes, peppers, aubergine and courgette, then add to mince mixture. Add seasoning and tin of tomatoes. Cook pasta and mix with other ingredients, placing in a casserole dish. Put cheese on top. Grill until lightly brown and serve with salad and garlic bread.

Camphill Blair Drummond.

Flemish Beef

2 lbs stewing steak	2 tsps thyme
3 - 4 onions, sliced	1 bay leaf
1 Tbsp vegetable oil	1 garlic clove, crushed
1 heaped Tbsp plain flour	Salt and freshly ground black
½ pint brown ale	pepper

Cut steak into 1 or 2 inch squares and sear in very hot oil, a little at a time, browning well before removing to a plate. Add the onions to the hot oil and fry until brown. Put meat and juices back into casserole, then add flour, lowering heat and stirring. Gradually add remaining ingredients. When simmering, stir well and cover with a tight fitting lid. Cook gently for 2 - 3 hours, without removing the lid until finished.

P. M. Oldfield, Middlesborough.

Stiphado - *Greek Stew, serves 4 - 6*

2 lbs rump steak	½ pint stock
4 Tbsps cooking oil	3 lbs small onions
¼ pint red wine	1 clove garlic, crushed
5 ozs tomato purée	Salt and pepper

Oven temperature: 310°F. 155°C. Gas mark 2.

Cut the steak into serving pieces and brown in cooking oil. Blend purée and stock, add wine and stir well. Place steak in casserole. Add onions and cover with liquid mixture. Season. Cook in a slow oven for 4 hours.

Audrey Cowan, Hamilton.

Creamy Mushroom Steak - *serves 4*

1 lb stewing steak, cubed	10½ oz tin condensed mushroom
1½ ozs butter	soup
3 ozs mushrooms, sliced	¼ pint milk
	Seasoning

Oven temperature: 310°F. 155°C. Gas mark 2.

Brown steak cubes in melted butter then add mushrooms and cook for 1 or 2 minutes. Mix soup and milk, adding to steak. Season. Put into a casserole dish, cover and place in centre of oven, baking for about 2½ hours until tender.

Mairi Black, Rutherglen.

Beef Soufflé

½ lb lean roast beef
Salt and pepper
3 egg yolks
4 egg whites
Shallot

For the sauce:
1 oz butter
½ Tbsp flour
1 Tbsp mushroom ketchup
1 teacup beef gravy
Worcester or anchovy sauce
Salt and pepper

Oven temperature: 350°F. 175°C. Gas mark 4.

To make the sauce, melt the butter and add the flour, cooking for 1 minute. Stir in gravy, ketchup, Worcester sauce and salt and pepper. Boil until it thickens.

Mince the beef. Mix with the sauce; season well with salt and pepper. Add the yolks. Put through a sieve and mix in chopped shallot to taste. Fold the stiffly beaten egg whites in lightly. Pour into a soufflé dish, lay a paper over the top to prevent burning, and bake for 20 minutes.

Kathleen Montgomery, Aberdeen.

Stuffed Liver

1 lb liver
2 ozs dripping
½ pint sage and onion stuffing
2 onions, finely sliced

2 ozs seasoned flour
1 beef cube made up with half
    amount of water

Oven temperature: 350°F. 175°C. Gas mark 4.

Dip slices of liver in flour and fry in dripping. Place in a greased dish. Make up stuffing and put 1 Tbsp on each piece of liver. Fry onions and put on top. Put the flour in the frying pan and add the made up beef cube, stirring until thick. Pour gravy over the liver. Cover and cook for 1½ hours in the oven. Thin gravy with water if it is too thick.

Kathleen Montgomery, Aberdeen.

Liver and Leek Casserole - *suitable for slimmers*

½ lb liver
1 medium leek, chopped

1 10 oz tin tomatoes
¼ lb mushrooms, chopped

Oven temperature: 310°F. 155°C. Gas mark 2.

Put liver in a casserole dish. Add leek, tinned tomatoes and mushrooms. Put
in the oven for about 1 hour until tender.

Staff, Eastern General Hospital, Edinburgh.

Haggis

½ lb rindless bacon, finely chopped
½ lb liver, finely chopped
1 sheep's heart, finely chopped
½ lb pork sausage meat
½ lb uncooked rice

½ Tbsp sage and onion stuffing
mix
1 large onion, chopped
Salt and pepper

Finely chop bacon, liver and heart. Mix all ingredients together thoroughly.
Place in a floured cloth and steam for 3 hours in a very large saucepan. Leave a
big pleat in the cloth before you tie it up to leave plenty of room for the haggis
to swell. *When it begins to boil, make for door as you never know what is going to
happen when it swells!*

Kathleen Montgomery, Aberdeen.

Chops Americaine

4 thick lamb chops
4 rashers bacon
3 large tomatoes

2 tsps Worcester sauce
Seasoning
1 Tbsp oil

Oven temperature: 350°F. 175°C. Gas mark 4.

Arrange chops in a shallow baking dish. Top with bacon, skinned and sliced
tomatoes, sauce, seasoning and oil. Bake in the oven until tender. Serve with
green salad.

Kathleen Montgomery, Aberdeen.

Sauerbraten - *Braised Beef marinated in Vinegar*

1 lb beef or lamb	Juniper berries, optional
Salt and pepper	½ pint vinegar
2 onions, chopped	1 pint water
1 garlic	Oil or margarine
2 – 3 bay leaves	Flour or cornflour
2 – 3 ground cloves	Wine or lemon juice, optional

Rub salt and pepper onto the meat. Put in a bowl, add the onions, garlic, bay leaves, ground cloves and juniper berries. Cover the meat with the vinegar and water, then marinate with the lid on for 2 – 3 days. Dry meat on kitchen paper. Heat up the oil or margarine in a pot and fry the meat until crispy. Add the sieved marinade to it and cook slowly for 1½ hours. Thicken the gravy with flour and add the wine or lemon juice if required.

Adelheid Stutz (Germany), Camphill Blair Drummond.

Leek and Potato Bake - *serves 4*

1 tsp oil	*For the cheese sauce:*
2 leeks, finely chopped	1 oz butter
4 ozs streaky bacon, chopped	1 oz plain flour
1 lb potatoes, sliced and cooked	½ pint milk
Parsley to garnish	1 tsp mixed mustard
	6 ozs Cheddar cheese, grated
	Salt and black pepper

Heat oil in a small saucepan and fry the leeks and bacon until soft. Place in the bottom of a casserole dish and arrange the potatoes on top. Make the cheese sauce by melting butter in a saucepan, adding the flour and cooking for 1 minute. Gradually stir in the milk and bring to the boil. Remove from heat. Stir in the mustard and 4 ozs of cheese and season. Pour sauce over the potatoes and sprinkle with remaining cheese and grill until golden brown. Serve hot, garnished with parsley.

Jean Simpson, Grangemouth.

Tiroles Grostel - *Potato dish with Eggs, Ham and Cheese*

3 ozs ham and fat mixed
1 onion
Fat for frying
½ lb left over meat or sausages
1 lb potatoes, boiled and sliced

Salt and pepper
2 eggs
3 Tbsps milk
Grated cheese

Fry the ham and onion in hot fat and add the chopped meat or sausage. Add the potatoes and season. Cook for 10 minutes, stirring occasionally. Mix the eggs and milk together and pour over the mixture, then sprinkle cheese on top. Serve with salad.

For vegetarians, this can be made into a satisfying meal by omitting meat and adding more vegetables and cheese.

Renate Seubert, (Germany), Camphill Blair Drummond.

Spaghetti alla Carbonara

4 eggs
5 ozs fresh single cream
8 ozs streaky bacon, chopped
1 oz butter

12 ozs spaghetti
6 oz cheddar cheese, grated
Salt and pepper
2 Tbsps fresh parsley

Beat together the eggs and cream. Fry the bacon in butter until crisp. Meanwhile cook spaghetti in boiling salted water until tender, but not too soft. Drain and add to bacon. Cook for 1 minute, stirring all the time. Remove from the heat and add the egg mixture. Mix well – the heat of the spaghetti will be enough to cook the eggs. Stir in 4 ozs of cheese and season. Transfer to serving dish and serve immediately, sprinkled with parsley and remaining cheese.

Pat Scott, Edinburgh.

Starrs Super Supper Bake

1 small cauliflower
2 large leeks
8 ozs honey roast ham

1 pint cheese sauce
Breadcrumbs
2 ozs cheese, grated

Boil the cauliflower florets until just soft. Boil slices of leek until soft. Place in an ovenproof dish along with sliced honey roast ham, each slice rolled up. Cover with cheese sauce and sprinkle with breadcrumbs and cheese. Crisp under the grill for a few minutes.

Lisa Starrs, Edinburgh.

Baked Gammon and Pineapple

2 gammon steaks
1 small tin pineapple
Cinnamon

For the sauce:
1 oz margarine
1 oz flour
¼ pint milk
¼ pint pineapple juice
1 Tbsp parsley, chopped

Oven temperature: 350°F. 175°C. Gas mark 4.

Trim the rind from gammon and place steaks in a baking dish. Cover with slices of pineapple and sprinkle with cinnamon. Pour over juice from pineapple. Cover and bake for 1 hour.
To make the sauce, melt margarine in a pan, add the flour and then milk and juice from steaks. Add chopped parsley. Serve steaks on hot dish, garnish with pineapple. Serve sauce separately.

Muriel Gilray, Edinburgh.

Pork Parcels - *serves 4*

4 ozs long grain rice
5 ozs frozen peas
5 ozs frozen sweetcorn
4 spring onions, chopped

Salt and pepper
4 pork chops
1 Tbsp soy sauce
4 Tbsps cider

Oven temperature: 350°F. 175°C. Gas mark 4.

Cook rice and put in a basin. Cook peas and sweetcorn for 2 minutes, add to rice, chops, onions and season mixture. Cut 4 large squares of foil and put a chop in the middle of each. Sprinkle well with soy sauce. Put ¼ mixture on top of each chop and add a spoonful of cider. Wrap into a parcel and place in a roasting tin. Bake in the oven for 40 minutes. Serve direct from the foil onto serving plates. Suitable for freezing.

Mary Downie, Killin.

Sweet and Sour Pork Chops

3 Tbsps soft brown sugar
4 tsps dry mustard
Salt and black pepper
6 pork chops

1 Tbsp lemon juice
1 tin tomatoes
4 stuffed olives, optional
4 gherkins, optional

Oven temperature: 350°F. 175°C. Gas mark 4.

Measures level. Mix brown sugar, mustard, salt and pepper. Put chops onto a roasting tin or heatproof dish and sprinkle dry mustard over them, followed by lemon juice. Pour tin of tomatoes around chops. Slice olives and gherkins and scatter on top. Bake in the oven for 40 – 45 minutes.

Muriel Gilray, Edinburgh.

Cornish Ham Pudding *- serves 4*

6 thin slices white bread
1½ ozs butter
3 thick slices cooked ham
3 tomatoes, thinly sliced

3 eggs
Salt and pepper
1 pint milk

Oven temperature: 350°F. 175°C. Gas mark 4.

Remove crusts from bread and spread with butter. Place slices of ham on three slices of bread, top with tomato slices, reserving some for garnishing. Cover with remaining bread slices, buttered side up. Cut each sandwich into four triangles. Place in a shallow, buttered, ovenproof dish. Beat together eggs, salt and pepper, then milk. Strain over bread and garnish with remaining tomato. Bake in the oven for 35 – 40 minutes until custard has set.

Mary Downie, Killin.

Aberdeenshire Pie - *serves 2*

½ lb potatoes
½ lb cooking apples
½ lb onions
4 ozs bacon
Salt, pepper and sugar
Water

For the pastry:
3 ozs flour
1½ ozs fat
Salt and cold water

Oven temperature: 375°F. 190°C. Gas mark 5.

Grease pie dish and pre heat oven. To make short crust pastry, sieve the flour and salt into a bowl, cut and rub in fat until like breadcrumbs. Add only enough cold water to make a stiff dough.
Peel potatoes, apples, onions and slice thinly. Roll sliced apples in sugar. Dice bacon. Place layers of apples, onions and bacon in pie-dish, in that order, finishing with a layer of potatoes. Season each layer well. Pour in a little water. Roll pastry 1 inch bigger all round than top of pie-dish. Cut off strip and place around the edge of dish. Wet it and put on lid of pastry. Decorate edges and make 2 slits in lid. Bake for 1 – 1¼ hours. Tomatoes can also be added to filling if desired.

Mairi Black, Rutherglen.

Duck with Black Cherries

1 roasting duck
1 large onion, chopped
1 medium tin black cherries

Salt, pepper and sugar
Cornflour
Port wine or sweet sherry

Roast the duck the day before the dish is required. Pour off the fat and chill. Fry onion until soft, then add cherries, reserving the juice. Cook until soft. Add the 'duck juice' and most, or all, of the black cherry juice. Add salt, pepper and a little sugar. Boil up. Thicken with cornflour, mixed with port wine or sweet sherry. De-bone the duck and add to the sauce. Heat up well for serving.

Lord James Douglas-Hamilton, M.A., LL.B., M.P..

Turkey in Honey and Ginger - *serves 4*

1 Tbsp vegetable oil	Salt and freshly ground black
2 ozs clear honey	pepper
2 Tbsps Dijon mustard	4 turkey breasts, skinned
1 tsp ground ginger	Watercress to garnish

Oven temperature: 350F. 175°C. Gas mark 4.

Preheat oven. Heat oil in a flameproof casserole just large enough to take 4 turkey portions in a single layer. Stir the honey, mustard and ginger into the oil. Remove from heat and season to taste. Arrange the turkey pieces in the mixture in the casserole, and turn to coat them. Bake for 30 minutes, basting occasionally. Turn the turkey portions and continue to cook for 30 minutes, basting until tender. Garnish with watercress. Serve with boiled brown rice.

Rhoda Burdis, Brampton.

Petti di Pollo Gratinati - *Chicken Breasts baked in Breadcrumbs, serves 6*

6 fresh chicken breasts, boned	*For béchamel sauce:*
1 large egg, beaten	1 pint milk
4 ozs fresh dried breadcrumbs	1 small onion
2 ozs butter	1 small carrot
6 Tbsps vegetable oil	Piece of celery
4 ozs Gruyère cheese, thinly sliced	1 bay leaf
Salt and freshly ground black	peppercorns
pepper	2 ozs butter
	1½ ozs flour
	Salt

Oven temperature: 430°F. 220°C. Gas mark 7.

Dip each chicken breast in the egg, then the breadcrumbs and shake off any excess. Heat the butter and oil in a frying pan and when hot, cook the chicken breasts in a single layer. Turn them over when they are brown and fry the other side. Drain on absorbent kitchen paper.

To make the béchamel sauce, place the onion, carrot, celery, bay leaf and peppercorns in the milk, heat until boiling and then leave to cool for 5 minutes. Strain. Melt the butter in a pan, add the flour, then mix in the milk. Put the chicken in a large buttered ovenproof dish and cover with the sauce. Place sliced Gruyère on top. Bake in the oven for 10 – 15 minutes until a golden crust forms on the top. Allow to settle for about 5 minutes before serving. Recommended serving with courgettes.

Christine Kinnear, BBC Radio Scotland.

Chicken in Orange Sauce

1½ oz butter	1 chicken stock cube
2 Tbsps oil	4 sprigs fresh tarragon or 1 Tbsp
4 chicken quarters or breasts	dried
1 large onion, chopped	¼ oz cornflour
6 oz can frozen orange juice	5 oz carton soured cream
¼ pint water	

Oven temperature: 350°F. 175°C. Gas mark 4.

Melt butter and oil in a flameproof casserole dish and brown chicken thoroughly on all sides and remove. Cook the onion for 2 – 3 minutes in the butter and oil. Stir in concentrated orange juice, water, stock cube and tarragon. Bring to the boil and add the chicken, cover with lid or foil and bake in the oven for 1 – 1½ hours, until chicken is tender. Remove chicken, skim off any excess fat, blend cornflour with 2 Tbsps water and add to sauce. Return to boil and cook for 2 – 3 minutes stirring continuously, cool slightly and stir in soured cream. Replace chicken. Serve decorated with fresh tarragon or parsley. Recommended to serve with rice or boiled potatoes and braised celery.

Moira Cousins, Glasgow.

Chicken with Prunes

4 chicken pieces	1 clove garlic, crushed
1½ tsp salt	3 oz prunes
1 oz butter	½ pint water
1 Tbsp oil	1½ Tbsps cornflour

1 medium onion, chopped   1 tsp honey
2 carrots, sliced

Oven temperature: 330°F. 165°C. Gas mark 3.

Sprinkle chicken with some salt. Brown slowly in the melted butter and oil in an ovenproof casserole. Add onion and fry until soft. Add carrots, garlic, prunes and water. Bring to simmering, cover and cook on hob for 30 minutes or in oven for 45 minutes. Sprinkle on remaining salt and the cornflour and thicken. Stir in honey.

Mrs. E. Ormiston, Inverary.

Chicken and Ginger Vegetable Casserole

3 Tbsps oil   Flour
1 carrot, diced   1 apple, cored and quartered
1 onion, diced   ¼ pint *Crabbie's* Green Ginger wine
4 oz mushrooms   2 ozs butter
8 chicken pieces   Freshly chopped parsley

Oven temperature: 400°F. 205°C. Gas mark 6.

Heat oil and lightly fry carrot, onion and mushrooms. Remove from pan and put in the bottom of a casserole dish. Coat chicken pieces in flour, brown gently in the frying pan then place on top of the vegetables. Add apple to dish and pour over ginger wine. Cook in the oven for 20 – 30 minutes. When cooked through, place chicken on a serving dish, lift the vegetables with a slotted spoon and place on top of the chicken. Boil the remaining liquid and whisk in the butter. Pour over the chicken and vegetables and garnish with parsley.

Stuart Barber, "L'Aperitif," Edinburgh.

Chicken and Orange Casserole

4 chicken thighs or breasts   ¼ pint milk
3 Tbsps flour   Finely grated rind and juice of
2 ozs butter   1 orange

2 ozs finely chopped onion
2 rashers bacon, chopped
½ pint chicken stock

1 level Tbsp finely chopped capers
Salt and pepper
Orange and parsley to garnish

Oven temperature: 330°F. 165°C. Gas mark 3.

Toss chicken in flour until well coated. Heat butter, then add chicken and fry until brown on both sides, then place chicken in a casserole. Sauté onion and bacon for 5 minutes, then stir in excess flour and cook for 2 - 3 minutes. Add stock and milk all at once and bring to the boil, stirring continuously. Add orange, capers and salt and pepper, then pour this mixture over the chicken. Cover and cook for about 1½ hours. Garnish with fresh orange segments and parsley. Freezes very well.

P. M. Oldfield, Middlesborough.

Chicken in Mushroom Cream Sauce

4 – 6 chicken portions
½ pint fresh single cream
10½ oz tin condensed mushroom
  soup

2 cloves garlic, crushed
Salt and pepper
Paprika

Oven temperature: 350°F. 175°C. Gas mark 4.

Preheat oven. Arrange chicken in a shallow baking dish. Blend together the cream and mushroom soup, then add garlic, salt and pepper. Spoon sauce over chicken. Dust with paprika and bake, uncovered, until chicken is tender.

Archie McPherson, B.B.C.

Pineapple Chicken Casserole

4 chicken joints
Seasoned flour
2 Tbsps corn oil
1 large onion, diced

1 green pepper, deseeded and sliced
4 ozs mushrooms, sliced
1 chicken stock cube
8 oz tin pineapple

Oven temperature: 350°F. 175°C. Gas mark 4.

Coat the chicken joints witth a little seasoned flour and fry in oil until golden brown. Transfer to casserole. Fry onions, pepper and mushrooms. Dissolve stock cube and make upto 1 pint with pineapple juice. Add to pan and simmer for 2 – 3 minutes, then pour mixture over chicken joints. Add pineapple. Cook in the oven for 1 hour or until chicken is tender. Serve with rice.

Staff, Eastern General Hospital, Edinburgh.

Chicken à la Cuisinière - *serves 10*

2 Tbsps oil
10 chicken joints
2 large onions, chopped
6 rashers streaky bacon, chopped
14 oz and 7½ oz tins peeled
   tomatoes

8 ozs mushrooms, sliced
1 bay leaf
Salt and pepper
2 Tbsps cornflour
1 glass sherry, optional

Oven temperature: 370°F. 190°C. Gas mark 5.

Heat 1 Tbsp oil in a pan and fry chicken until lightly browned. In a casserole heat the remaining oil and fry onions and bacon for a few minutes. Add tomatoes and mushrooms and bring to boil, stirring all the time. Add bay leaf, seasoning and chicken. Return to boil, then cover casserole and place in oven for 1 hour. Before serving, remove chicken and keep warm. Blend and add cornflour, then add sherry. Spoon over chicken. Serve with rice.

Mairi Black, Rutherglen.

Chicken and Macaroni Pudding

6 ozs macaroni
1 tsp cooking oil
12 ozs cooked chicken
½ oz butter

2 large eggs, well beaten
½ pint chicken stock
Salt and pepper

Put the macaroni in a pan of boiling salted water then add the oil. Cook for about 15 minutes until tender. Chop the chicken into small pieces. When the macaroni is cooked, drain thoroughly and run water through to remove excess starch. Turn into a bowl and add butter and let it melt. Stir in chicken, eggs, stock and salt and pepper. Put into a greased steaming bowl and steam for 1½ hours.

Kathleen Montgomery, Aberdeen.

Pasta Spirals with Chicken Sauce

12 ozs skinless chicken slices
1 medium onion, thinly sliced
4 ozs mushrooms, sliced
2 tsp tarragon, dried or fresh
12 ozs pasta spirals
1 Tbsp oil

1½ ozs butter
½ pint single cream
2 tsp white wine
Vinegar
Salt and pepper
Parmesan cheese, for serving

Slice chicken thinly. Chop tarragon if fresh. Bring a large saucepan of salted water to the boil. Meanwhile heat oil and butter in another pan to a medium heat. Cook pasta in boiling water. Fry onion until soft then add chicken slices and cook for 3 minutes. Add mushrooms and cook for a few minutes. Finally add the cream and tarragon and bring just to the boil. Remove from heat, gradually stir in the vinegar and season to taste. When the pasta is ready, drain and put into a warmed serving bowl. Pour the chicken sauce over the pasta and mix roughly. Serve immediately, accompanied by parmesan cheese.

Kathleen Montgomery, Aberdeen.

Oatmeal Fritters

2 Tbsps oatmeal
1 Tbsp S.R. flour
½ tsp baking powder

Pinch of salt
Milk
Fat for frying

Mix ingredients and add enough milk to make a creamy batter. Drop spoonfuls of mixture into hot fat and fry on both sides until crisp. Serve with bacon or sausages.

Pat Scott, Edinburgh.

Salads, Vegetables and Vegetarian

Carrot and Mandarin Salad

2 lbs carrots, grated   1 tin mandarin oranges

Grate carrots, stir in mandarin oranges and juice. Allow to stand, covered in fridge, for 1 – 2 hours before using.

Mairi Black, Rutherglen.

Cauliflower, Date and Banana Salad

1 cauliflower   ¼ pint good mayonnaise
2 ozs stoned dates, chopped   1 lemon, grated rind and juice
2 bananas, sliced

Break cauliflower into florets and steam for 5 minutes. Cool quickly. Mix mayonnaise, lemon rind and juice together. Combine all ingredients and serve in a large salad bowl. Flavours of this dish develop after a short time.

Jean Inglis, Edinburgh.

Cucumber and Yogurt Salad

1 cucumber, finely sliced   2 cloves garlic
French dressing   Salt, black pepper and sugar to taste
1 pot greek yogurt   1 tsp freshly chopped mint

Lay cucumber overlapping in dish either in rows or rings. Sprinkle a little french dressing over. Mix remaining ingredients well together and spoon over the cucumber. Garnish with a sprig of mint.

Amberley Carter.

Crunchy Salad

½ cauliflower, divided into sprigs   1 eating apple, cored and chopped
¼ cucumber, chopped   1 medium onion, chopped
¼ white cabbage, shredded   Garlic and garlic mayonnaise
¼ red cabbage, shredded

Rub salad bowl with garlic, add all prepared ingredients and bind together with 2 Tbsps garlic mayonnaise.

Mairi Black, Rutherglen.

Green Fruit Salad

1 large banana, sliced
Lemon juice and brown sugar to
     taste
1 small melon, chopped

2 medium green apples, cored
     and chopped
1 kiwi fruit, peeled and sliced
Greek yogurt

Slice the banana into lemon juice and add melon, unpeeled apples, and kiwi fruit. Add sugar if wished. Chill and serve topped with Greek yogurt.

Elizabeth Aitken, Aberdeen.

Orange and Watercress Salad - *serves 4 - 6*

3 oranges
1 bunch watercress
2 ozs black olives
Mustard and cress to garnish

For the dressing:
1 small onion, finely chopped
1 Tbsp fresh parsley, chopped
3 Tbsps vegetable oil
1 Tbsp wine vinegar
¼ tsp mustard powder
Pinch of sugar, salt and finely
     ground black pepper

Using a sharp knife, cut in a spiral motion to remove the peel and pith from the oranges. Cut into slices. Arrange the watercress in a shallow serving dish, place the orange slices in 2 overlapping lines down the centre of the watercress. Arrange olives down the centre of each line of orange slices. Cover and refrigerate until required.
Just before serving, make the dressing, by putting the ingredients into a screw top jar with salt and pepper to taste. Shake well until blended. Pour the dressing around the salad, garnish with mustard and cress, if liked, and serve at once.

Rhoda Burdis, Brampton.

Something Different - *savoury jelly*

1 red jelly   Beetroot
1 Tbsp vinegar

Make up the red jelly, but substitute vinegar for 1 Tbsp of measured water. Dice beetroot and set in jelly. This is also successful using a lime jelly and thinly sliced cucumber.

Mairi Black, Rutherglen.

Dutch Salad

1 cooked beetroot   French dressing with mustard
2 cooked potatoes   6 anchovy fillets
1 heart celery   Watercress

Cut the beetroot, potatoes and celery into strips. Mix lightly with the dressing and pile in a salad bowl. Decorate with strips of anchovy fillet and small bunches of watercress.

Kathleen Montgomery, Aberdeen.

Red Witch Salad

4 ozs radicchio (Italian red lettuce)   *For the dressing:*
   divided into leaves   1 Tbsp virgin olive oil
3 sticks celery, chopped   1 Tbsp lemon or lime juice
2 large carrots, grated   1 tsp mustard
1 cup fresh bean sprouts   2 tsps chopped fresh basil
3 ozs chicory, divided into leaves   Black pepper
1 avocado, peeled and sliced
4 spring onions, chopped finely

Keeping out 8 radicchio leaves and 5 leaves of chicory, mix all salad ingredients in a bowl. Mix ingredients for dressing in a screw top jar by shaking well. Pour dressing over salad and toss well. Arrange radicchio and chicory around a platter in a sunburst pattern. Place rest of salad in centre of dish.

Jean Inglis, Edinburgh.

Ham Salad with Pineapple

½ lb cooked ham   Mayonnaise or salad dressing
1 small fresh or tin pineapple   Sliced gherkins

Cut the ham into short strips. Dice pineapple. Toss lightly with sauce or
dressing. Garnish with gherkins.

Kathleen Montgomery, Aberdeen.

Rice Salad

Rice   Cucumber, chopped
Tomatoes, chopped   Natural yogurt
Eggs, hard boiled   Mayonnaise
Cheese, cubed   Garlic, crushed
Chives, chopped

Boil some salted water in a saucepan then add rice and cook. Strain and put
into a bowl. Add hard boiled eggs and cheese. Make a dressing with natural
yogurt, mayonnaise, chives and a very little garlic. Mix all remaining
prepared ingredients with the rice and stir through the dressing.

Mhairi Black, Camphill Blair Drummond.

Devilled Potato Salad

2 lb new potatoes   3 sticks celery, sliced
1 Tbsp apple cider vinegar   ½ pint sour cream
Sea salt and pepper   ¼ pint mayonnaise
3 apples, diced   Pinch of curry powder
3 slices streaky bacon, chopped and   1 Tbsp chopped parsley
    cooked crisply

Boil new potatoes in skins until just tender. Drain, peel and slice. Toss in cider
vinegar, season with salt and pepper. Allow to cool. Add apples, celery and
bacon. Blend sour cream, mayonnaise, curry powder and lemon juice and
toss potato mix in this sauce. Sprinkle with chopped parsley.

Jean Inglis, Edinburgh.

Herring Salad - *a good starter or main dish*

2 salted or pickled herrings	1 – 2 apples
4 – 5 boiled potatoes	Salt and white pepper
1 pickled cucumber	Beetroot juice
1 – 2 Tbsp onion, chopped	7 Tbsps whipped cream
2 – 3 pickled beetroots	Crisp lettuce to serve

If herrings are salted, soak overnight. Cut all ingredients into uniform pieces and mix everything together. Either pack into a mould and chill before turning out or use individual dishes. Serve on a bed of crisp lettuce. Garnish with parsley or chopped egg.

Pat Scott, Edinburgh.

Fish Salad

Cold cooked fish	1 lettuce
Salt and pepper	1 lemon
A little tartare sauce or mayonnaise	

Use cold cooked fish divided into large flakes. Season and mix with sauce and shredded lettuce. Decorate a dish with the crisp inner lettuce leaves and slices of lemon, then arrange the fish on the dish.

Kathleen Montgomery, Aberdeen.

Georg's Special Fritters

Porridge	Milk
Flour	Mixed vegetables, optional
Eggs, beaten	Salt and pepper

Use cold porridge and add flour and eggs to bind, plus some milk to keep mixture fluid. Add salt and pepper, and cooked vegetables if desired. Fry in hot frying pan. Ready cooked meat may also be added.

Georg Schad, Camphill Blair Drummond.

Ribbles - *a Wintertime supper dish*

White fat
Oats
Hazel nuts, chopped and roasted
Almonds or walnuts

Sultanas or raisins
Sugar to taste
Milk

Oven temperature: 220°F. 100°C. Gas mark ¼.

Melt fat in a flat pan in the oven. Cover bottom of pan with oats and cook gently, turning occasionally, until slightly brown. After cooking, add hazel nuts, almonds, sultanas and sugar. Serve with milk.

Sally Schad, Camphill Blair Drummond.

Hummus

8 ozs chick peas
4 pints water
2 cloves garlic, crushed
½ lemon

¼ pint natural yogurt
Salt and pepper
Paprika to garnish

Soak peas overnight. Strain and bring to boil in the water and cook for 3 – 4 hours. Strain and purée the peas with the garlic. Add juice of the lemon and yogurt. Smooth into a serving dish and garnish with paprika if required. Serve with wholemeal rolls and side salad.

Mrs. E. Ormiston, Inverary.

Baked Avocado with Spinach, Mushrooms and Tomato Ginger Sauce

2 ozs butter
4 ozs mushrooms, sliced
1 tsp ginger, finely grated
1 clove garlic, crushed
1 lb spinach, blanched

For the sauce:
1 oz margarine
4 ozs onion, finely chopped
1 clove garlic, chopped
1 tsp fresh or ground ginger

Salt and pepper
2 ripe avocados
2 ozs Cheddar cheese

1 oz flour
2 ozs tomato purée
1 tsp oregano
1 bayleaf
¾ pint chicken or vegetable stock
Small glass *Crabbie's* green ginger wine

Oven temperature: 450°F. 235°C. Gas mark 6 – 8.

Melt butter in a pan, add mushrooms, ginger and garlic. Cook gently for a few minutes and add well drained spinach. Season to taste.

To make the sauce, melt margarine in a small pan, add onion, garlic and ginger, then brown slightly. Add flour and cook gently for a few more minutes. Mix in tomato purée, oregano and bayleaf. Cool slightly then add stock and *Crabbie's* ginger wine. Stir carefully until the sauce starts to boil then simmer gently for 20 minutes. Correct seasoning if required.

Split avocados in half lengthwise and remove a thin slice from the base so that they will sit firmly. Place on a buttered ovenproof dish. Spoon in the spinach and mushroom mixture then coat with the tomato and ginger sauce. Sprinkle with Cheddar cheese and bake in the oven for 15 – 20 minutes.

Stuart Barber, "L'Aperitif," Edinburgh.

Stuffed Potatoes

3 potatoes
1 egg yolk
2 egg whites
1 Tbsp cheese

2 Tbsps milk
1 oz butter
1 tsp parsley
Salt and pepper

Oven temperature: 350°F. 175°C. Gas mark 4.

Scrub potatoes and bake. Cut in halves. Scoop out potatoes into a pan, leaving skins intact. Add cheese, yolk, butter, milk and parsley. Season and heat. Beat egg whites stiffly and stir in. Fill skins with the mixture, piling high, brush with yolk and bake for 15 minutes.

Pat Scott, Edinburgh.

Vegetable Curry

3 Tbsps oil	1 tsp cummin seeds
2 medium onions	3 ozs creamed coconut, chopped
2 cloves garlic, finely chopped	1 medium cauliflower
4 green chilli	8 ozs carrots, thinly sliced
1 oz fresh ginger root, peeled and grated	2 medium courgettes, thinly sliced
2 tsps curry powder	2 green peppers
1 tsp turmeric	¼ pint basic vegetable stock

Cut the cauliflower into small florets. Core, de-seed the peppers and cut them into 1 inch strips. Core and de-seed and finely chop the chilli.

Heat the oil in a pan over a low heat. Mix in the onion, garlic, chilli and ginger and cook them until onions are soft. Stir in the curry powder, turmeric and cummin seeds. Cook for 1 minute more. Put the coconut in and stir until it melts. Fold in the vegetables. Pour in the stock and bring to the boil. Cover and cook on moderate heat for 20 minutes.

N.B. Creamed coconut comes in the form of a hard white block. It can be bought in most supermarkets and Health food shops.

Muriel Gilray, Edinburgh.

Stovies

Dripping	Potatoes, peeled and sliced
1 onion, sliced	Salt and pepper

Put some dripping into a strong pan and heat until smoking hot. Add the onion, or alternatively, add chopped syboes or shallots. Fry. Add potatoes and seasonings, then reduce heat. Cover closely and cook gently for an hour. When ready, stir up from the bottom with a strong basting spoon. If desired left over meat may be chopped andd added to stovies. The secret of good stovies is to cook the potatoes without burning and without lifting the lid during cooking.

Pat Scott, Edinburgh.

Celeriac and Tomato Bake - *serves 4*

1 lb celeriac, peeled and sliced	½ tsp dried thyme
Salt and pepper	3 ozs mature Cheddar cheese, grated
6 large tomatoes, skinned and	Freshly ground black pepper
thinly sliced	Oil for dressing

Oven temperature: 400°F. 205°C. Gas mark 6.

Put the celeriac into a saucepan of boiling salted water and boil for 5 minutes until just tender. Drain well. Starting with the celeriac, arrange in layers with the tomato, in a lightly oiled ovenproof dish. Sprinkle each layer with thyme and about ⅓ of the cheese and salt and pepper to taste. Finish with a layer of celeriac and sprinkle with remaining cheese. Bake in the oven for about 30 minutes until the top is golden brown.

Serve as a light lunch or supper dish, or serve with a meat dish as a substitute for potatoes.

Rhoda Burdis, Brampton.

Tabboule - *serves 6 - 8*

2 – 3 ozs couscous, not cooked	2 Tbsps olive oil
1 lb tomatoes	1 – 2 Tbsps mixed herbs – lots of
1 lb peeled cucumber	mint, parsley, chives, tarragon,
1 white onion	etc.
Juice of 3 – 4 lemons	Salt and pepper

Coarsely grate tomatoes, cucumber and onion. Add lemon juice, olive oil, finely chopped herbs, salt and pepper. Mix thoroughly. Add couscous. Leave to swell for at least 3 hours in a cool place.

Marjory Curtis, Edinburgh.

Courgette and Lentil Gratin

4 ozs red lentils	*For the filling:*
1 Tbsp olive oil	8 ozs courgettes, diced

1 onion, chopped
1 Tbsp tomato purée
2 ozs oat flakes
1 Tbsp lemon juice
2 Tbsps parsley or mixed herbs

2 eggs, beaten
1 Tbsp wholemeal flour
2 fl ozs milk
Seasoning
2 ozs grated cheese

Oven temperature: 430°F. 220°C. Gas mark 7.

Cook lentils in 8 fluid ozs of water until soft. Beat well. Heat oil and fry onion. Add lentils, tomato purée, herbs, oats and lemon juice. Press into a greased 8 inch flan.
To make the filling, steam courgettes until tender. Blend eggs with flour and add milk, stir in courgettes and season. Spoon filling into case, cover with cheese and bake for 20 – 25 minutes.

Muriel Gilray, Edinburgh.

Courgette and Tomato Pie - *serves 4*

3 Tbsps olive oil
2 onions, sliced
1½ lbs courgettes, sliced
2 cloves garlic, crushed
6 tomatoes, skinned and chopped
1 Tbsp tomato purée
Salt and pepper

For the topping:
1½ lbs potatoes, boiled and mashed
4 spring onions, finely chopped
2 Tbsps olive oil
4 Tbsps milk

Oven temperature: 400°F. 205°C. Gas mark 6.

Heat oil a in pan, add onions and courgettes and fry for 10 minutes, stirring occasionally. Add garlic, tomatoes, tomato purée and seasoning. Cover and simmer for 5 minutes. Turn into a 2½ pint ovenproof dish.
For the topping, beat potatoes with spring onions, oil, milk and salt and pepper. Spoon over courgette mixture to cover. Cook in a pre-heated oven for 30 – 40 minutes until golden.

Betty Smeaton, Newcastle upon Tyne.

Vegetarian Moussaka

2 aubergines – approx 14 ozs
Salt
6 ozs lentils
1 vegetable stock cube
1 large onion, chopped
1 green pepper, chopped
4 Tbsps vegetable oil

4 ozs mushroooms, sliced
1 tsp ground cummin
1 tsp marjoram
14 oz tin tomatoes, drained
4 potatoes, cooked and mashed
2 eggs, beaten
¾ pint white sauce

Oven temperature: 350°F. 175°C. Gas mark 4.

Slice the aubergine and layer on a plate sprinkling liberally with salt to extract bitter juices. Cook lentils in 1 pint of boiling water and the stock cube for approximately 25 minutes until all the moisture has been absorbed. Fry the onion and pepper in the oil for a few minutes, add the mushrooms and spices then cook for a further 2 minutes. Add this to the lentils and mix in the tomatoes.

In the pan used for the onions etc., fry the rinsed aubergine slices using more oil if necessary. Layer the lentil mixture with the aubergine slices in a 4 pint ovenproof casserole. Top with the mashed potato and pour over a mixture of beaten egg and white sauce. Cook in the oven for 25 minutes until the topping is slightly browned.

Elizabeth Aitken, Aberdeen.

Spinach Layer Loaf - *serves 4*

10 oz packet frozen spinach
1 large onion, finely chopped
4 ozs mushrooms, finely chopped
4 ozs peanuts, chopped
6 ozs wholemeal breadcrumbs

7 ozs cheese, grated
4 ozs frozen sweetcorn
3 large eggs, beaten
3 Tbsps vegetable oil

Oven temperature: 350°F. 175°C. Gas mark 4.

Thaw the spinach as instructed on the packet. Fry the onion and mushrooms for 5 minutes in oil. Add the peanuts and cook for 1 minute more. Remove from the heat and add the breadcrumbs, cheese and sweetcorn. Mix well and allow to cool. Add the egg and mix until stiff. Put slightly less than half of this in a well greased 2 lb loaf tin and layer with the spinach on top, finishing with the rest of the breadcrumb mix. Cook for 25 minutes in the oven. Serve on its own or with salad or homemade tomato sauce.

Elizabeth Aitken, Aberdeen.

Onion, Mushroom and Tomato Flan

For wholemeal shortcrust pastry:
8 ozs wholemeal S.R. flour
2 ozs vegetable cooking fat
2 ozs margarine
Pinch of salt

For the filling:
1 oz butter or margarine
3 medium onions, chopped
¼ lb mushrooms, chopped
1 large tomato, chopped
1 large egg, beaten
Salt and pepper
½ tsp oregano, or other herb

Oven temperature: 350°F. 175°C. Gas mark 4.

To make the pastry, rub fat into the flour and mix with water to a manageable dough. Roll this out and line a 9 inch flan dish; suggest baking for 10 minutes before adding the filling.
To make the filling, melt the margarine in a pan and sauté the onions, mushrooms and tomato. Pour this mixture into a basin and allow to cool slightly, before adding the egg and seasoning. Stir well, then pour into pastry case and bake in oven for 30 – 40 minutes until set.

Betty Smeaton, Newcastle upon Tyne.

Leek and Noodle Bake

4 ozs wholewheat noodles
1 large onion, sliced
1 large leek, sliced
Vegetable oil
2 eggs, beaten

¼ pint milk
Salt, black pepper
Mixed herbs
3 ozs grated cheese
Cayenne pepper

Oven temperature: 330°F. 165°C. Gas mark 3.

Boil the noodles until soft. Gently fry the onion and leek in a little oil until soft. Put beaten eggs in basin and add milk, salt, pepper and mixed herbs. Mix drained noodles into onion and leek mixture and place in a gratin dish. Pour over the mixture of egg and milk. Sprinkle with grated cheese and cayenne pepper. Bake for 30 minutes.

Jean Inglis, Edinburgh.

Cheese, Rice and Tomato - *a favourite for children*

Rice	Cheddar cheese, grated
Salt and pepper	Breadcrumbs
Tomatoes	Butter

Oven temperature: 350°F. 175°C. Gas mark 4.

Boil the rice in salted water for 12 minutes. Rinse under a cold tap and set aside. Cut up the tomatoes and set aside. Butter an ovenproof dish and layer it with the rice, then tomatoes and season to taste with salt and pepper, then the grated cheese. Repeat the layers: rice, tomatoes, seasoning, cheese. Top with the breadcrumbs, dot with butter and place in the oven for about 30 – 40 minutes.

Tam Dalyell, M.P.

French Onion Pie - *serves 4 - 6*

For the pastry:	*For the filling:*
6 ozs flour	1½ lbs onions, sliced
3 ozs fat	1 Tbsp sugar
½ tsp salt	3 Tbsps oil
3 Tbsps water	6 ozs Cheddar cheese
	3 eggs, beaten
	2 Tbsps milk
	½ tsp salt

Oven temperature: 400°F. 205°C. Gas mark 6.

To make the pastry mix together flour and salt, then rub in the margarine. Add water to form a stiff dough, then roll out and line a dish. Mix together onions and sugar, then cook in oil. Stir in remaining ingredients and place in pastry case. Bake for 40 minutes.

Sally Schad, Camphill Blair Drummond.

Käs Spätzle - *Cheese Pasta*

12 ozs flour	Salt
½ pint warm water	Nutmeg
3 Tbsps semolina	Onions, chopped
6 eggs	Cheese, grated

Oven temperature: 350°F. 175°C. Gas mark 4.

Mix together the flour, water, semolina and eggs, then whisk thoroughly. Season the dough with salt and nutmeg. Fry the onions and set aside. Boil some salted water in a large pot. Drop teaspoons of the dough directly into the boiling water and let the dumplings boil for a few minutes. Put them into an ovenproof dish together with the fried onions and cheese. Bake for about 20 minutes. Serve with lettuce or tomato sauce.

Renate Seubert (Germany), Camphill Blair Drummond.

Bean Roast with Tomatoes

½ lb butter or haricot beans	1 tsp mixed herbs
1 onion, sliced	1 Tbsp parsley, chopped
½ lb margarine	Salt and pepper
2 eggs, well beaten	Flour
½ cup breadcrumbs	1 lb small ripe tomatoes

Oven temperature: 350°F. 175°C. Gas mark 4.

Soak beans overnight, then cook in slightly salted water together with the onion, until beans are soft. Mash and put the mixture into a basin, and add 2 ozs of the margarine and the eggs, breadcrumbs, herbs and seasoning. Mix well together. Turn onto a floured board. Shape into a neat block and dredge with flour. Place on a well-greased baking tin with remainder of margarine in small lumps on top. Place whole tomatoes round the savoury. Bake for about 30 minutes in the oven, basting occasionally. When nicely browned, serve with a brown gravy and apple sauce. If preferred, this roast can be eaten cold with salad.

Kathleen Montgomery, Aberdeen.

Nut and Lentil Roast

4 ozs lentils, cooked
4 ozs ground walnuts
Seasoning, mace or parsley
1 Tbsp grated onion
1 egg, beaten

2 ozs cooked macaroni, chopped
Stock or brown/soy sauce
Butter
Breadcrumbs

Oven temperature: 350°F. 175°C. Gas mark 4.

Mix together the lentils, walnuts, macaroni, seasoning and onion. Bind with the egg and enough stock or sauce to moisten. Form a neat roll, sprinkle with breadcrumbs and roast in the oven for about 1 hour, basting with a little butter if necessary. Serve with any sauce preferred.

Sarah Scott, Broughty Ferry.

Walnut Roast

1 teacup ground walnuts
1 teacup cold potatoes, mashed
1 small onion, chopped
1 tsp mixed herbs

Egg
1 teacup brown wheaten
   breadcrumbs
Butter

Oven temperature: 400°F. 205°C. Gas mark 6.

Mix together the walnuts, potatoes, onion and herbs. Bind with egg. Sprinkle with breadcrumbs and pieces of butter. Bake in the oven until brown. Serve with vegetables and gravy.

Sarah Scott, Broughty Ferry.

Walnut Cutlets

1 onion, chopped
3 ozs lentils
3 ozs rice
2 ozs walnuts, grated
2 ozs cheese, grated

3 ozs breadcrumbs
A little marmite or similar
    flavouring
Salt

Oven temperature: 400°F. 205°C. Gas mark 6.

Cook the onion, lentils and rice together in boiling water for approximately 20 minutes, then steam until thick and dry. Mix everything together and form into cutlets. Fry in deep fat or bake in the oven. Serve with onion rings.

Sarah Scott, Broughty Ferry.

Potato Pastry - *for flans or pasties*

½ lb plain flour
1 tsp salt

5 ozs margarine
½ lb cooked potato, mashed

Mix together the flour and salt then rub in the margarine. Combine with cold mashed potato and mix to a firm dough with cold water. Knead and roll out thickly.

Sarah Scott, Broughty Ferry.

Lentil Walnut Burgers - *makes 5 large burgers*

1½ cups dry lentils
4 ozs fresh mushrooms
1 small green pepper
1 stalk celery
1 small carrot
2 cloves garlic
1 small onion
1 cup walnuts
Butter

1 tsp salt
Black pepper
1 tsp chilli powder
½ tsp dry mustard
¼ cup raw rolled oatflakes
5 Tbsps tomato paste
2 eggs, beaten
Worcester sauce
Cheddar cheese, optional

Soak and cook the lentils until tender. Dice finely the mushrooms, pepper, celery, carrot, garlic, onion and walnuts then sauté in butter with salt, black pepper, chilli and mustard. Combine sauté with lentils and rolled oatflakes. Mash moderately, but not so much that vegetable chunks are lost. Add tomato paste, beaten eggs and a dash or two of Worcester sauce. Mix well. Form into large fat patties. Chill for 1 hour. Grill or fry in butter. Suggest Cheddar cheese on top.

Rebecca Thomson, South America.

Spinach Gnocchi - *Italian*

1 lb potatoes
1 lb fresh spinach
2 eggs
8 ozs ricotta or cream cheese
4 ozs butter

Salt and pepper
¼ tsp ground nutmeg
2½ – 3 ozs semolina
1 oz parmesan, grated

Oven temperature: 400°F. 205°C. Gas mark 6.

Boil the potatoes and when cooked, peel and wash them without adding more liquid. Meanwhile mash the spinach and cook it without adding any extra water. Drain, squeezing out as much liquid as possible and chop finely. Mix the potatoes and spinach with all the ingredients except for parmesan and half the butter. Chill for 45 minutes. Preheat the oven. Bring a large pan of salted water to the boil. To cook the gnocchi, drop a teaspoon of the mixture into the pan, a few at a time. Keep the water boiling. The gnocchi are done when they rise to the surface. Remove them. Melt the remaining butter and pour it over the gnocchi. Sprinkle the parmesan over and bake for 10 minutes.

Ulrike (Austria), Camphill Blair Drummond.

Vegetable Risotto - *serves 4*

2 Tbsps olive oil
8 ozs brown rice
2 large courgettes, cubed
2 onions, sliced
2 carrots, cubed

6 ozs mushrooms, sliced
1 tsp each of cummin, coriander,
    paprika and garam masala, all
    crushed
4 ozs Cheddar cheese, grated

1 pepper, chopped
Leeks, aubergine, etc, optional
2 cloves garlic

Salt and pepper
2 ozs raisins
Toasted nuts, optional

Oven temperature: 350°F. 175°C. Gas mark 4.

Heat oil in a pan and fry the spices. Add all the vegetables except for the mushrooms and cook gently for about 10 minutes. Add rice and mushrooms and stir well. Add salt, pepper and raisins. Pour in 1¾ pints of boiling water. Bring to boil and place in a covered dish in the oven for about 45 minutes, until water is absorbed. Serve with grated cheese on top.
This recipe can be made with any seasonal vegetables. The spices are optional. Toasted nuts may be added at the end.

Averill Marks, St. Andrews.

Pease Pudding

8 ozs split peas
Pinch of salt
1 ham bone
1 oz butter

1 egg. beaten
1 tsp mixed herbs
Seasoning

Wash the peas well, then soak overnight. Tie the peas loosely in a cloth, then place in a saucepan with salt, hambone and enough water to cover. Boil for 2 - 3 hours. Remove bag and sieve or blend the peas. Add the butter, egg, herbs and seasoning to taste. Beat until well mixed, tie in a floured cloth and boil for a further 30 minutes. Turn onto a hot plate and serve.

Pat Scott, Edinburgh.

Potatoes Lyonnaise - *serves 3 - 4*

2 ozs butter
2 medium onions, finely sliced

8 boiled potatoes

Fry the onions in melted butter until brown and crisp. Remove and place in a hot dish. Slice the potatoes coarsely and fry until brown. Drain well and mix with onions.

Pat Scott, Edinburgh.

SNACKS AND
SAVOURIES

Devilled Ham Spread

4 ozs ham, minced
2 ozs soft margarine
2 tsps Worcester sauce

Seasoning
¼ tsp mustard

Cream ham and margarine. Stir in remaining ingredients. Spreads eight large slices of bread.

Kathleen Montgomery, Aberdeen.

Roes on Toast

¾ lb cod roe
Salt and pepper

1 bacon rasher, chopped
4 rounds of toast

Wash and dry the roes. Dip in seasoned flour and fry in hot fat. Chop the bacon and add when almost cooked. Serve piled on buttered toast.

Kathleen Montgomery, Aberdeen.

Salmon Boats - *makes 36*

18 large slices white bread
Soft margarine for coating

For decoration:
3 tomatoes
Cocktail sticks

For the filling:
1 oz soft margarine
1 oz flour
½ pint milk
Salt and pepper
4 oz tin salmon
¼ green pepper, chopped

Oven temperature: 350°F. 175°C. Gas mark 4.

Pre-heat the oven. Grease 36 patty tins with melted margarine. Remove the crusts from bread then flatten with a rolling pin. Cut 2 circles to fit patty tins from each slice. Press into greased tins. Brush over each bread lining with melted margarine. Bake 15 – 20 minutes until crisp and pale gold in colour. For the filling, put the margarine, flour, milk and seasonings in a pan and whisk over a moderate heat until thick. Remove the skin and bones from the salmon, and add to the sauce, with chopped pepper. Fill into cases. Make

tomato sails and fix into filling with cocktail sticks.
Do not put the filling in until time for using. The cases on their own keep for days in an airtight tin.

Mairi Black, Rutherglen.

Cheese Dreams

Cheddar cheese	Seasoning
Margarine	Thinly sliced white bread

Oven temperature: 480°F. 250°C. Gas mark 9.

Pre-heat oven to maximum. Grate cheese and mix with margarine. Season well. Trim crusts off bread. If not very thin, use a rolling pin to flatten slices. Spread with cheese mixture and roll up like a Swiss roll, pressing to keep in position. Halve each roll. Put on a lightly greased tin and bake in the hottest oven possible for 8 – 9 minutes. Serve immediately.

Ena Barrie, Motherwell.

Sausage Whirls - *makes 30*

For the pastry:	*For the filling:*
2 ozs Cheddar cheese, grated	½ lb sausage meat
8 ozs S.R. flour	1½ Tbsps H.P. sauce
1 level tsp salt	1 egg
2 ozs margarine	½ level tsp salt
Scant ¼ pint milk	Pinch of mixed herbs

Oven temperature: 430°F. 220°C. Gas mark 7

Pre-heat oven. Grease 2 baking trays. Put flour and salt in a bowl then rub in margarine. Add cheese and milk, stirring with a fork until mixed. Turn out onto a floured board and knead lightly. Roll to rectangle 14 x 9 inches. Make filling by mixing all the ingredients together in a bowl, then spread onto dough, nearly to the edges. Roll up from one long side. Cut into ½ inch slices and put on trays. Bake for 15 minutes. Allow to cool before serving.

Mairi Black, Rutherglen.

Quick Quiche

3 eggs
2 ozs flour
2 – 3 slices bacon or ham, chopped

1 small pot fresh cream
2 ozs cheese, grated
½ pint milk

Oven temperature: 400°F. 205°C. Gas mark 6.

Mix all the ingredients together, adding the milk last. Pour into a well greased flan tin and bake on the middle shelf in the oven for 30 minutes.

Marjory Curtis, Edinburgh

Hawaiian Cheese Flan

For the pastry:
8 ozs plain flour
1 level tsp salt
2 ozs lard
2 ozs margarine
Cold water to mix

For the garnish:
8 oz can pineapple rings
12 cucumber slices

For the filling:
4 eggs
½ pint milk
2 level tsps salt
1 level tsp dry mustard
Pepper
6 ozs Cheddar cheese, grated

Oven temperature: 370°F. 190°C. Gas mark 5.

Pre-heat the oven and grease a 11 x 7 inch Swiss roll tin.
Make the short crust pastry, roll out and line the tin. Press pastry into the corners and up the sides. Roll off surplus.
To make the filling, beat the eggs, milk and seasoning together in a bowl. Sprinkle half the grated cheese over the base of the flan case. Pour egg mixture into flan and sprinkle with remaining cheese. Bake in the centre of oven for 35 – 40 minutes until the filling is set and pastry is golden brown. Cool. Cut flan into 12 pieces.
Drain syrup from pineapple. Cut each ring into 6 wedges. Cut each cucumber slice from edge to centre and form a twist. Put cucumber twist on each piece of flan and arrange a wedge of pineapple at either side of each cucumber twist.
Undecorated flan can be wrapped in cling film and stored in the fridge for

up to 3 days, or wrapped in foil and frozen for up to 2 months. Thaw overnight in fridge or heat flan in a moderate oven for about 30 minutes, then decorate as above with pineapple and cucumber.

Mairi Black, Rutherglen.

Party Snack

8 ozs hard cheese, grated	1 Tbsp Worcester sauce
½ onion, chopped	3 Tbsps green pepper, chopped
3 Tbsps celery, chopped	Walnuts, finely chopped
8 ozs cream cheese	Crushed pineapple, optional

Mix all ingredients in a bowl except for the walnuts. Pat into a ball and roll out in the finely chopped walnuts. Keep in fridge. Slice off chunks and eat with crackers. If using crushed pineapple, use less cream cheese accordingly.

Pat Scott, Edinburgh.

Bread Bouchées - *makes 8*

4 slices white bread, 1 inch thick	2 ozs prawns or 1 hard boiled egg
Melted margarine	together with 2 grilled rashers of
½ oz soft margarine	bacon
½ oz flour	1 tsp chopped parsley
¼ pint milk	1 tsp tomato purée
Seasoning	

Oven temperature: 400°F. 205°C. Gas mark 6.

Pre-heat the oven and grease a baking tray. Using a 2 inch plain cutter, cut 2 rounds from each slice of bread, then carefully remove the centres of each round with a 1½ inch plain cutter, but DO NOT cut through the bottom of rounds. Brush top and sides of each round with melted margarine and bake for 10 – 15 minutes.
Put the margarine, flour, milk and seasoning in a small pot and whisk over a moderate heat until thick. Mix remaining ingredients and add to the sauce. Fill bread bouchées and serve hot.

Mairi Black, Rutherglen.

Liptauer Cheese Spread

4 ozs cream cheese	Seasoning
2 ozs soft margarine	¼ tsp paprika
3 anchovy fillets, chopped	¼ tsp mustard
3 gherkins, chopped	

Beat together cheese and margarine until smooth, then add the anchovies, mustard and gherkins. Season well and beat in the paprika. Spreads eight slices of bread.

Kathleen Montgomery, Aberdeen.

Vienna Cheese Turnovers - *makes 16*

½ lb frozen puff pastry	2 ozs raisins
3 oz packet 'Philly' cheese	1 oz almonds, skinned and chopped
2 tsps caster sugar	Beaten egg or milk
2 ozs peel, chopped	Icing sugar

Oven temperature: 430°F. 220°C. Gas mark 7.

Pre-heat oven, grease a baking tray and thaw the pastry.
Roll out the pastry into a 12 inch square and divide into 16 pieces. Beat together the remaining ingredients except almonds and icing sugar, then place 1 teaspoonful in the centre of each square of pastry. Dampen edges of pastry slightly and fold each corner to centre, overlapping and sealing edges. Place on the baking tray. Brush with beaten egg or milk. Sprinkle with chopped almonds. Bake for 15 minutes. Dust with icing sugar 3 minutes before end of cooking.

Mairi Black, Rutherglen.

Egg à la Dijon

4 eggs, hard boiled	2 ozs cooked mushrooms
Tomatoes for garnish	Seasoning
4 ozs cooked ham	

Cut the eggs in halves, remove the yolks and cut small thin slices off the bottom of each half to allow them to stand properly. Make a purée of the minced or chopped ham and mix with egg yolks and mushrooms and seasoning. Fill the whites with mixture. Garnish with tiny pieces of tomato.

Kathleen Montgomery, Aberdeen.

Sausage Potatoes

2 potatoes   2 sausages

Oven temperature: 350°F. 175°C. Gas mark 4.

Scrub potatoes and core a hole through the centre. Fill with sausage. Bake in the oven until potato is soft.

Pat Scott, Edinburgh.

Target Tangs - makes 15

1 small French loaf, about 15 inches   6 ozs red Leicester cheese, grated
Butter   3 ozs full fat soft cream cheese
4 ozs cooked ham, 4 slices   1 tsp Worcester sauce
6 gherkins   ½ level tsp salt
½ small onion, chopped   Pepper

With a sharp knife cut through crust at one side of the loaf to its centre. Open out and scoop out inside, leaving only a border of dough. Make 2 ozs bread dough into crumbs. Butter inside of loaf. Line with 2 slices of ham. Place 3 gherkins lengthwise along 1 side of each remaining slice of ham. Roll up firmly. Put onion in a bowl with grated cheese, cream cheese and breadcrumbs, sauce, seasoning and 2 ozs butter. Mix well with wooden spoon. Spread half of mixture into hollowed loaf, arrange gherkin rolls down centre and spread remaining mixture on top. Press loaf firmly together. Wrap tightly in foil and chill before serving. Cut into 1 inch slices to serve.
This loaf can be stored, wrapped in foil, in a fridge for up to 4 days or up to 2 months in a freezer. Just before serving remove foil and place in a hot oven to crispen.

Mairi Black, Rutherglen.

Devilled Crescents - *makes 8*

¾ lb cooked ham, chicken or
   corned beef
2 level Tbsps pickle
1 Tbsp water

1 small packet frozen puff pastry,
   just thawed
Milk

Oven temperature: 430°F. 220°C. Gas mark 7.

Pre-heat the oven and grease a baking tray. Remove any fat from meat and cut into small pieces. Put in bowl, add pickle and water. Mix. Roll out pastry into a circle of 12 inch diameter and cut across 4 times to make 8 triangles. Place a little of filling in centre of base of each. Roll up triangle from base and bend to form crescent, then brush with milk and bake for 10 minutes. Serve hot.

Mairi Black, Rutherglen.

Cheese Scones

4 ozs plain flour
½ tsp salt
1 oz margarine
Cayenne pepper
1 level tsp cream of tartar
½ level tsp Bicarbonate of Soda
1 – 2 ozs cheese, grated
4 Tbsps milk to mix

For the filling:
2 ozs chopped pork
½ oz onion, chopped
1 Tbsp tomato sauce
Mixed herbs, optional
1 level Tbsp margarine
Egg or milk to glaze

Oven temperature: 350°F. 175°C. Gas mark 4.

To make the filling, chop up meat and onion and mix all ingredients thoroughly. Set aside. Make scones by sieving flour and rubbing in the margarine until like breadcrumbs. Mix to a light elastic dough with milk and add remaining ingredients. Turn onto a floured board and knead lightly. Roll out to a 10 inch square and cut into four. Divide filling into four and place in the centre of each square. Damp all edges and fold like an envelope. Glaze and bake for 10 – 15 minutes.

Kathleen Montgomery, Aberdeen.

Coffee Mac

1 measure *Crabbie's* green ginger
   wine
½ measure whisky

Coffee
Double cream
Crushed chocolate flake

Pour ginger wine and whisky into a large stemmed glass. Top with hot, strong coffee, leaving ¼ – ½ inch gap at the top. Gently pour double cream over the back of a teaspoon or carefully pipe with aerosol cream. Sprinkle with crushed chocolate flake and serve immediately.

Stuart Barber, "L'Aperitif", Edinburgh.

Apple and Raspberry Frappé - *a cool summer drink*

2 sweet apples
½ tsp lemon balm or mint, finely
   chopped

½ cup fresh raspberries
Spring water, optional
Ice cubes, optional

Core the apples and chop into small pieces, leaving skins intact. Place all ingredients together in a blender and liquidise, add spring water to thin if wished. Add ice cubes if wished.

Jean Inglis, Edinburgh.

Childrens' Party Punch

6 oz cherry jelly
2 cups boiling water
½ cup sugar
¼ tsp salt

4 cups orange juice
¾ pint ginger ale
¾ cup lemon juice

Dissolve jelly in boiling water, then add sugar and salt, stirring well. Add orange juice, followed by ginger ale and lemon juice. Serve chilled.

Pat Scott, Edinburgh.

Favourite Punch

2 cups double strength tea
½ cup sugar
2 cups cold water
½ cup grape juice

1 cup orange juice
⅓ cup lemon or lime juice
½ pint ginger ale

Prepare tea and add sugar, stirring until dissolved. Stir in remaining ingredients.

Pat Scott, Edinburgh.

Orangeade

4 oranges, grated rind and juice
3 lemons, grated rind and juice
2 ozs citric acid

6 lbs granulated sugar
4 pints boiling water

Grate the fruit skins, add the acid and sugar, then scald with boiling water. When cool, add the juice of oranges and lemons. Leave to stand for 24 hours before straining and bottling.

Pat Scott, Edinburgh.

SAUCES AND
PRESERVES

To Preserve a Husband

Select with care – young and green varieties take longer to prepare but often are excellent when done. Those too crusty take a long time to cook tender. One neither hard nor soft gives best satisfaction. Do not keep in a pickle nor in too hot water nor prick to test tenderness as this leaves a mark. Even poor varieties may be made sweet and tender by this method.

Wrap in a mantle of charity and keep warm over a steady fire of loving domestic devotions.

Garnish with patience, sweeten with smiles, flavour with kisses to taste. Serve with peaches and cream.

Thus prepared they will keep for years.

E. Barrie, Motherwell.

Home made Sauce

2 cups vinegar
1 Tbsp treacle
1 Tbsp sugar
½ Tbsp cornflour
½ tsp salt

½ tsp mustard
1 tsp mixed spice and cayenne
   pepper
Pepper to taste

Put all ingredients in a saucepan, carefully stirring until coming to the boil. Boil briskly for a few minutes. Remove from heat and allow to cool. Bottle when cold. The cayenne may be omitted if desired.

Kept carefully corked, this will keep for a few months.

Edith McDougall, Edinburgh.

Tomato Sauce *- for pasta and other dishes*

1 medium onion, chopped
1 green pepper, chopped
Vegetable oil
14 oz tin tomatoes

Pinch of mixed herbs
1 clove garlic, optional
1 Tbsp tomato purée

Fry the onion and pepper in vegetable oil with the herbs and garlic. Add the tomatoes and tomato purée. Simmer for 15 minutes.

To this sauce can be added: sliced courgette; mushrooms; grated carrot; celery; or almost any vegetable to make a complete meal with pasta and grated cheese.

Elizabeth Aitken, Aberdeen.

Glaze for Baked Ham *- sugarless*

2 Tbsps 'Whole Earth' sugarless
  Apricot Jam

1 tsp powdered mustard
Grated rind and juice of orange

Mix together and spread over ham before baking

Maggie Sherriff, Blair Drummond.

Salad Dressing

½ Tbsp dry mustard
1 heaped tsp plain flour
½ cup vinegar
½ cup sugar

½ cup milk
2 eggs, well beaten
Pinch of salt
1 Tbsp butter

Mix mustard and flour together in a pan, gradually add vinegar and stir well. Add all other ingredients. Stir constantly over a low heat but do not boil.

Audrey Cowan, Hamilton.

Rowan Jelly from Glenfeshie *- for Christmas turkey or any red meat or game*

Rowan berries
Crab apples

Sugar
Water

Pick almost ripe rowan berries and crab apples. Put in a pan with just enough water to cover. Boil until soft. Strain overnight, then put back in the pan with 1 lb sugar to each pint juice. Boil rapidly for 30 minutes. Crab apples give a good colour.

Moira Cousins, Glasgow.

Mint Jelly

6 lbs cooking apples, quartered
2 pints water
2 pints vinegar

2 ozs mint, chopped
1 lb sugar per pint of juice

Place apples in a saucepan with water, vinegar and mint, then simmer until apples are cooked. Strain through a muslin. Measure the juice and return to pan with appropriate amount of sugar. Stir until the sugar dissolves, then bring to the boil, boiling until a good set is reached. Pot and cover.

Sadie McQueen, Balvicar.

Apple Chutney

7 lbs green apples
4 lbs brown sugar
1 lb preserved ginger, chopped
2 lbs sultanas
1 medium onion, chopped

1 tsp cayenne pepper
1 tsp pickling spice
1 tsp salt
2 pints vinegar

Peel and slice the apples, then boil with the sugar and a little water until fairly thick. Add ginger, sultanas, onion and spices then boil for 20 minutes. Add vinegar and simmer until mixture is thick. Put into jars. Cover while hot.

Pat Scott, Edinburgh.

Rhubarb Chutney

4 lbs rhubarb
6 medium onions, chopped
1 lb apples, peeled and chopped
1 lb raisins, chopped
1 lb brown sugar

½ oz cayenne pepper
1 oz curry powder
2 tsps salt
1 pint malt vinegar

Wipe rhubarb and cut into small pieces, then add all remaining ingredients. Bring to the boil and simmer until chutney is a deep, dark brown. Put into warm pots and keep for several weeks before using.

Ena Barrie, Motherwell.

Quick Uncooked Chutney

1 large green pepper
1 large red pepper
2 lbs cooking apples, peeled, cored
  and grated
1 lb onions, grated
1 lb carrots, grated

4 ozs raisins
Juice of 1 lemon
4 ozs dark brown sugar
2 level tsps salt and black pepper
2 level tsps paprika
6 drops Tabasco sauce

Halve and de-seed the peppers, and chop for 10 seconds in a food processor with a double-bladed knife attachment, or coarsely grate by hand. Mix in all remaining ingredients. Put into jars. This makes 4 lbs of chutney which will keep for at least 3 weeks if stored in a fridge.

Lemon Cheese

3 ozs butter
6 ozs granulated sugar
3 eggs, beaten

Juice and rind of 2 small
  lemons

Melt butter, sugar and lemon in a double boiler. Add beaten eggs to the hot mixture. Heat and stir gently until thick, about 10 – 15 minutes. Pour into small pots. This can be kept in a fridge, but not for very long.

Anne Carter, St. Andrews.

Citrus Curd

Grated rind and juice of 1 orange
Grated rind and juice of 1 lemon
Grated rind and juice of 1 lime
8 ozs sugar

3 ozs butter, cut into small pieces
1 egg
4 egg yolks

Put the fruit juices and rind, sugar and butter in a pot and cook over a gentle heat for 3 minutes until sugar is completely dissolved. Pour into a bowl and cool for 5 minutes. Beat the egg yolks and the egg together, then strain into juice mixture, beating continuously. Cook mixture in the bowl over hot water for 5 minutes, or until it begins to thicken and will coat the back of a spoon. Pour into heated jars. This will fill 4 small jars.

Raspberry Jam - *microwave*

1 lb frozen raspberries   1 lb sugar
2 Tbsps lemon juice

Microwave: 650 watts. High setting.

Place the frozen fruit in a large bowl and microwave on high for 4 minutes to thaw. Stir several times with a wooden spoon to ensure even thawing. Add lemon juice and sugar. Mix well and microwave on high for 5 minutes until sugar is dissolved. Stir several times during cooking. Microwave on high for 13 minutes stirring occasionally until setting point is reached. Pot and cover. Yields 1½ lbs of jam.

Mairi Black, Rutherglen.

Rhubarb and Orange Jam

4 lbs rhubarb   5 lbs sugar
2 oranges   1 lb raisins
1 lemon

Cut fruit, sprinkle with sugar and add raisins, then mix with a wooden spoon and leave for 1 hour. Bring to the boil, stirring to ensure sugar is dissolved. Cook slowly for 45 minutes. Stir until the liquid has evaporated from the fruit and the jam is thick. Test. Do not boil hard. Fill warm jars with hot jam, then cover with wax rings and put on lids immediately. Store in a dry cupboard. Yields 7 lbs.

Lockhart McEwan, Rutherglen.

Rhubarb, Apricot and Pineapple Jam

3½ lbs rhubarb, cut   1 pint water
5 lbs sugar   16 oz tin pineapple pieces
1 lb dried apricots

Cut rhubarb and cover with the sugar, then leave for 24 hours. Also, cut apricots and soak in water, leaving for 24 hours. Put all into a jelly pan with the pineapple pieces. Boil for 20 minutes, stirring, as it thickens quickly.

Mairi Black, Rutherglen.

Marmalade

2 lbs marmalade oranges   6 lbs sugar
1 lemon

Wash fruit and cut across in half. Put in a jelly pan and cover with water. Boil for 1 hour until soft and pulpy. Remove pips and put in a small saucepan, cover with water and bring to the boil. Mince fruit using a liquidiser or food processor. Measure fruit and juice from pan and water from pips and make up to 4½ pints. Bring to the boil and stir in sugar. Boil for 20 – 25 minutes and test. Yields 10 – 11 lbs.

Mairi Black, Rutherglen.

Mincemeat

2 oz almonds, chopped   12 ozs sultanas, chopped
2 ozs raisins, chopped   4 ozs mixed peel
8 ozs currants, chopped   1 orange, grated rind and juice
1 carrot, peeled and chopped   12 ozs demerara sugar
8 ozs chopped suet   ¼ pint brandy or rum
4 ozs apple, chopped   1 tsp mixed spice

Mix all ingredients together, cover and leave for 2 days, stirring occasionally. Bottle and label. Use within 3 months. Makes 4 – 5 lbs.

PUDDINGS

Stir-up Sunday

Stir up, we beseech thee
The pudding in the pot,
And when we get home,
We'll eat it all hot!

Choirboys' Rhyme.

Clootie Dumpling

3 ozs flour
3 ozs breadcrumbs
3 ozs chopped suet
1 tsp ground cinnamon
2 ozs sultanas
½ tsp ground ginger or nutmeg

2 ozs currants
2 tsps bicarbonate of soda
2 ozs brown sugar
1 Tbsp syrup
¾ cup sour milk or buttermilk
Caster sugar for serving

Mix together all the dry ingredients, except for caster sugar. Mix to a soft consistency with the milk. Dip a pudding cloth in boiling water and, using it all, dredge well with flour. Set it in a basin and spoon in the mixture. Tie ends well with a string, leaving space for swelling. Place a plate on the bottom of a steaming pan containing enough water to completely cover the dumpling. Simmer for 2 hours, ensuring it does not boil dry. Turn onto a hot ashet. Dredge with caster sugar and serve.

Pat Scott, Edinburgh.

Apple Dumpling

8 ozs S.R. flour
4 ozs suet
4 ozs sugar
1 large apple, chopped

Handful of raisins
Squeeze of lemon juice
1 egg, beaten
Milk

Mix all ingredients witth enough milk to make a soft dough. Steam in a covered basin for 2½ – 3 hours.

Sarah Scott, Broughty Ferry.

Half Pay Pudding

4 ozs flour	2 ozs brown sugar
4 ozs suet or margarine	1 oz mixed peel
4 ozs raisins	1 tsp ginger
4 ozs currants	2 tsps baking powder
4 ozs breadcrumbs	1 Tbsp treacle
½ pint milk	1 egg

Mix all ingredients together and steam in a covered basin for 3 hours.

Jean Inglis, Edinburgh.

Dampfnudeln - *Delicious Yeast Dumplings*

For the dough:

1 lb flour	Pinch of salt
½ pint warm milk	¾ oz yeast
3 ozs butter	3 ozs sugar
2 egg yolks	1 Tbsp vanilla sugar

For the sauce:

2 ozs butter	½ pint milk
	1 Tbsp sugar

Prepare a soft dough. Form dough balls with a spoon and let them rise on a tray.

To make the sauce: warm the butter and sugar and put in the milk. Put in the yeast dumplings and close the lid of the pot properly, then simmer for 30 minutes. Do not open the lid. The dumplings will be crunchy on the bottom. Reduce heat slowly until completely turned off. After 2 minutes open the lid, and only then. Serve dumplings on a warmed plate with fruit or vanilla sauce.

Renate Seubert (Germany), Camphill Blair Drummond.

Klatkager - *Rice Fritters*

Cold boiled rice	Almonds, chopped
2 eggs	2 Tbsps flour

Raisins   Butter
Lemon rind, grated   Sugar and jam to serve

Mix all the ingredients together. Drop in spoonfuls into a hot buttered frying pan. Fry on both sides. Sprinkle with sugar. Serve with jam.

Henriette Nicolaisen, Denmark.

Pineapple and Hazelnut Pudding

5 ozs margarine   Few drops of vanilla essence
5 ozs sugar   3 Tbsps milk
2 eggs   4 tinned pineapple rings
6 ozs S.R. flour   4 ozs hazelnuts

Oven temperature: 350°F. 175°C. Gas mark 4.

Butter the base of a 7 inch cake tin or ovenproof dish and arrange the pineapple and nuts on the bottom. Cream the butter and sugar together until soft and light. Whisk eggs and beat gradually into butter mixture. Sieve flour and mix vanilla with milk. Fold the flour and milk alternately into the creamed mixture. Pour onto fruit. Bake in a moderate oven for 1 hour.

Mrs. E. Ormiston, Inverary.

Orange Cheesecake

5 ozs butter   1 egg
½ Tbsp syrup   Mandarin oranges
7 ozs digestive biscuits   Whipped cream
5 ozs icing sugar

Melt 2 ozs of butter and the syrup in a pan and add the crushed biscuits. Press into a tin or flan dish, lined with greased foil. Cream together remaining butter with icing sugar and egg. Spread this over the cooled biscuit base, then place in fridge overnight. Top with mandarin oranges shortly before serving and then add whipped cream.

Marjorie Macleod, Newcastle-under-Lyme

Raspberry Cheesecake

2 ozs butter or margarine
1 Tbsp syrup
6 ozs digestive biscuits, crushed
2 eggs, separated
4 ozs caster sugar
Grated rind and juice of 1 lemon

½ tsp vanilla essence
8 ozs cottage or cream cheese
¼ oz gelatine
2 Tbsps water
8 ozs raspberries, or other fruit
Whipped cream

Melt butter with syrup and stir in the crushed biscuits. Spread in an 8 inch loose bottomed cake tin and leave until set hard. Beat the egg yolks and sugar in a bowl over hot water until light and fluffy. Add the lemon and vanilla then beat until the mixture cools. Add the cheese and gelatine, whisking until almost set. Beat the egg whites until stiff and fold into the mixture. Pour mixture onto biscuit base and leave to set. Decorate with fruit and cream.

Sadie MacQueen, Balvicar.

Lemon Meringue Pie

Grated rind and juice of 2 lemons
2 large eggs, separated
1 tin *Nestle's* condensed milk

1 pastry case
Caster sugar

Oven temperature: 310°F. 155°C. Gas mark 2.

Stir together the egg yolks, lemon and condensed milk, then put in the pastry case. Whisk the egg whites until stiff and spread on top. Sprinkle over a little sugar. Place in the oven until pale brown.

A note from Mrs. Mack: "This recipe is utterly 'yummy', it is my favourite pudding. You have never tasted anything as good in your *PUFF*. The Minister is only allowed it on Christmas Day."

Gwyneth Guthrie, 'Take the High Road', T.V. Personality.

Butterscotch Pudding

For the pastry base:
8 ozs flour

For the filling:
2 egg yolks

4 ozs margarine
1 egg yolk
Pinch of salt
1 oz caster sugar

2 Tbsps S.R. flour
1 cup soft brown sugar
1 cup water
2 Tbsps butter
1 tsp vanilla essence

Oven temperature: 370°F. 190°C. Gas mark 5.

Make the pastry and line a flan dish. To make the filling, mix the yolks, flour and sugar, add water and butter. Stir over a low heat until thick. Add the vanilla essence. Place the mixture into pastry case and bake in oven for about 30 minutes.

Kathleen Montgomery, Aberdeen.

Thing *- serves 6 - 8*

2 ozs margarine
2 ozs sugar
6 ozs digestive biscuits
16 oz tin pineapple chunks
15½ oz tin sliced peaches

1 egg white
3 Tbsps concentrated orange juice
3 ozs caster sugar
1 family block ice cream

Melt margarine and 2 ozs of sugar and add the crushed biscuits. Press into a shallow 7½ inch square tin, lined with foil. When firm, remove from tin and place on a plate.
Drain the fruit and arrange on the biscuit base, reserving some for decoration. Whisk together the egg white, orange juice and caster sugar in a bowl over hot water until mixture thickens. Place ice cream on top of fruit and cover with topping mixture. Decorate. Keep in freezer until served.

Mairi Black, Rutherglen.

Banana and Toffee Pie

8 ozs short crust pastry
1 large tin condensed milk
3 – 4 large bananas

½ pint double cream
2 level tsps instant coffee

Oven temperature: 370°F. 190°C. Gas mark 5.

Roll out pastry and cook blind in a flan dish for approximately 20 minutes. Allow to cool. Place unopened tin of condensed milk in a large saucepan of cold water and cover. Bring water to boil slowly and simmer for 2 hours, keeping the tin well submerged in water the whole time. Allow tin to cool. When cool, open tin. The condensed milk should have turned to a pale brown toffee consistency. Spread toffee onto pastry and slice bananas onto toffee. Whip the cream until thick and add coffee to it until well mixed in. Spread cream over toffee mixture and serve.

Blair Drummond.

Apple Pancakes

4 ozs flour
¼ pint milk
½ Tbsp olive oil
Pinch of salt
½ glass water

2 eggs
2 – 3 apples
Lemon juice
1 tsp caster sugar
Rum or Brandy, optional

Make a pancake batter with the flour, oil, salt, milk, water and eggs. Stir it very well, then let it rest for several hours.

Peel the apples and cut them into very thin slices. Sprinkle with a little caster sugar and a squeeze of lemon juice. Heat a small frying pan and coat with a thin film of oil or butter. Drop in a Tbsp of the batter and let it spread out as much as possible. On top of the pancake place 2 slices of apple, cover them with a little more of the batter and turn the pancake over. Let it cook a little longer than an ordinary pancake because of the apples. Serve flat, sprinkled with sugar. The apples can be soaked in a little rum or brandy.

George Younger, M.P.

Salzburger Nocken

3 ozs butter
6 ozs sugar
7 eggs, separated

1 oz flour
½ pint milk

Oven temperature: 350°F. 175°C. Gas mark 4.

Cream together the butter and sugar, then add the beaten egg yolks to the creamed mixture. Mix the unbeaten egg whites and flour into the mixture. Heat the milk in a dish and put the mixture into the milk. Bake in the oven until lightly brown, then with a spoon, form big 'Nocken' and serve immediately.

Ulrike (Austria), Camphill Blair Drummond.

Austrian Dessert

1 medium tin condensed milk	Salt
6 ozs flour	3 ozs sugar
3 eggs, separated	5 ozs butter

Oven temperature: 400°F. 205°C. Gas mark 6.

Mix well together the milk, flour, egg yolks, salt and half the sugar. Melt 2 ozs of the butter and whisk the egg whites. Fold these into the mixture. Melt remaining butter in a dish. Put the mixture into the dish with the butter, and place in a pre-heated hot oven, cooking until slightly browned. Crumble with two forks. Serve with remaining sugar on top.

Ulrike (Austria), Camphill Blair Drummond.

Bread Pudding - *a German Winter dish*

1½ lbs old bread in slices	Juice of 1 lemon
1 – 1½ pints milk	8 – 10 ozs fruit (apples, cherries)
2 – 3 eggs	Nuts and raisins, optional
Cinnamon, cloves and vanilla	Butter
Sugar or honey	

Oven temperature: 370°F. 190°C. Gas mark 5.

Soak the bread for a few hours in the milk, then mash it. Mix in the eggs, spices, sugar and lemon and add more liquid if too dry. Mix in the finely chopped fruit and, if you like, grated nuts and raisins. Grease an oven proof dish and put in the pudding mixture. Put some small flakes of butter on the top and bake for 45 minutes. Recommended to serve with fruit or vanilla sauce.

Camphill Blair Drummond.

Banana and Tapioca Sponge - *serves 6*

6 bananas, not over ripe
2 – 4 ozs sugar
¼ pint water
Juice of ½ lemon

1 pint milk
2 ozs tapioca
2 – 3 egg whites

Slice bananas and cook for 5 – 10 minutes to a purée with the sugar and water. Add strained lemon juice and beat to a smooth cream. Boil the milk and sprinkle in the tapioca, cooking gently for about 15 minutes, stirring all the time. Add banana purée, taste and sweeten if necessary. Whisk egg whites stiffly and fold lightly into the mixture. Stir lightly until cool and serve piled in a glass dish. Chill if desired.

Kathleen Montgomery, Aberdeen.

Pineapple Pudding

4 ozs margarine
4 ozs flour
1 pint milk
1 large tin pineapple pieces

4 ozs sugar
4 eggs, separated
6 ozs caster sugar

Oven temperature: 330°F. 165°C. Gas mark 3.

Melt the margarine and add the flour. Gradually add the milk stirring over heat until it makes a smooth sauce. Add pineapple juice and 4 ozs of sugar. Heat again. Add egg yolks and pour mixture into a dish. Whisk the egg whites until stiff and add half the caster sugar. Whisk again until stiff and add remaining sugar, folding in. Spread over sauce. Bake for about 30 minutes until brown. Cool and serve.

Sarah Scott, Broughty Ferry.

Apple Delicious

6 ozs cooking apples
4 ozs sugar
4 ozs butter

1 cup soft brown sugar
½ cup flour

Oven temperature: 350°F. 175°C. Gas mark 4.

Peel and slice the apples, then place in an ovenproof dish with sugar. Cream the butter and soft brown sugar, add the flour and spread the paste over the apples. Bake for 40 minutes in the oven. Serve hot with cream.

Staff, Eastern General Hospital, Edinburgh.

Old Fashioned Bread Pudding

12 ozs bread, including crusts
4 ozs shredded suet
2 ozs caster sugar
6 ozs mixed fruit
1 oz chopped candied peel

1 level tsp mixed spice
1 level Tbsp golden syrup
1 egg
1 oz demerara sugar

Oven temperature: 370°F. 190°C. Gas mark 5.

Cut up the bread and soak in cold water overnight. Empty bread into a colander and squeeze by hand or with a potato masher, pressing out as much water as possible. Place in a mixing bowl and using a fork, beat out any lumps then add the suet, sugar, dried fruit, peel and mixed spice. Stir in the syrup and egg, mixing thoroughly. Turn mixture into a greased shallow baking tin. Spread evenly and sprinkle the top with demerara sugar. Bake in the centre of the oven for 1 hour. Turn out pudding, cool slightly and serve warm or cold.

Audrey Hale, Ayr.

Beaufort Biscuit Cake

4 ozs drinking chocolate
4 ozs butter or hard margarine
2 Tbsps golden syrup

1 Tbsp water
8 ozs Rich tea biscuits
Sultanas and almonds, optional

Melt together the chocolate, butter, syrup and water, but do not boil. Add the broken biscuits, sultanas and chopped almonds. Press into a tin with the back of a large cold spoon. Turn out when cold, cut into squares and serve with whipped cream.

Maggie Sherriff, Blair Drummond.

Celebration Meringue

4 ozs hazelnuts
4 egg whites
9 ozs caster sugar
Vanilla essence

½ pint double cream
15 oz tin of fruit or fresh fruit in
   season

Oven temperature: 370°F. 190°C. Gas mark 5.

Grease and line two 8 inch sandwich tins. Brown nuts under the grill, then
rub off skins and chop finely. Whisk egg whites until stiff, then whisk in the
sugar gradually. Fold in the vanilla and nuts. Divide mixture between tins and
smooth over. Bake for 30 – 40 minutes, then cool. Whisk cream until thick
and mix half of it with the well drained fruit, using this mixture to sandwich
the meringues together. Decorate with remaining cream and any extra fruit.

Pat Scott, Edinburgh.

Date and Nut Torte

3 eggs, separated
¼ tsp salt
½ cup brown sugar
½ tsp vanilla
⅓ cup flour

¾ cup nuts, chopped
1 tsp baking powder
1 cup dates, chopped
½ pint double cream

Oven temperature: 350°F. 175°C. Gas mark 4.

Grease and flour a 9 inch round tin. Beat egg whites with salt until stiff. Beat
egg yolks with sugar until thick. Mix in the vanilla, followed by the flour,
baking powder and nuts, then finally mix in the dates. Fold egg whites into
batter. Pour into greased tin and bake for 40 – 50 minutes. When cool, turn
upside down on a serving plate. The centre of the torte will fall slightly,
leaving a little ridge around the edge. Fill the top with lots of whipped cream,
mixed with an extra ¼ tsp of vanilla.

Rebecca Thomson, South America.

Lemon Souffle - serves 3.

2 ozs butter
1 cup sugar
2 eggs, separated

2 ozs S.R. flour
Grated rind and juice of 1 lemon
1 cup milk

Oven temperature: 350°F. 175°C. Gas mark 4.

Cream the butter and sugar. Add the egg yolks then beat in the flour, lemon rind and juice. Add milk and fold in the beaten egg whites. Put mixture into a buttered pie dish and place container in cold water. Bake for about 1 hour in the oven. Serve hot or cold.

Wilma Aitken, Aberdeen.

Vanilla Pudding

2 ozs cornflour
Knob of butter
2 ozs sugar

1 pint milk
1 egg, separated
Vanilla essence

Put cornflour, butter, sugar and milk in a saucepan and bring to the boil. Boil for 2 minutes stirring all the time. Remove from heat. Stir in the beaten egg yolk and a few drops of vanilla essence. Whisk egg white stiffly and fold into pudding. Serve hot.

Mhairi Black, Camphill Blair Drummond.

Semolina Mould - serves 6

2 pints milk
4 ozs semolina

3 ozs caster sugar
Flavouring

Rinse a thick saucepan, then heat the milk to boiling point. Sprinkle in the semolina, stirring continually. Boil gently stirring all the time until the grain is quite cooked and appears transparent when lifted on the back of a spoon. Add sugar and stir well. Pour quickly in a cold wet mould.

Flavouring: **Lemon or orange:** Infuse thin strips of rind with the milk during heating. Remove before adding the grain. **Coffee:** Add 1 Tbsp of coffee essence with the sugar. **Chocolate:** Melt 3 ozs of chocolate in the milk or blend 1½ ozs cocoa with some of the milk. Add rum, brandy, sherry or vanilla essence.

Mrs. Montgomery.

Ice Cream

4 egg yolks   1 pint double cream
4 Tbsps icing sugar   Flavouring

Beat together the egg yolks and icing sugar until creamy. Whisk the cream stiffly and add to mixture. Add flavouring: cocoa; vanilla; instant coffee; nuts; etc. Put mixture in a suitable container and freeze until stiff.

Lisbeth Nielsen (Denmark), Camphill Blair Drummond.

French Chocolate Ice Cream

12 ozs double cream   4 fl ozs water
6 ozs good chocolate, eg *Meunier* 3 egg yolks
2 ozs granulated sugar

Whip the cream, using a little single cream to lighten if wished. Place the chocolate in a liquidiser or blender, ready for use. Boil the sugar and water to a syrup and pour it instantly onto the chocolate pieces, turning the liquidiser to full until it all melts. Then add the egg yolks quickly. Turn the chocolate mixture into the cream and fold in gently. Place in freezer.

Amberley Carter.

Plum Ice Cream

1 lb plums, weighed without   8 ozs sugar
   stones. Victoria or any red skin ½ pint water
   variety   2 egg whites
Juice of ½ orange   ¼ pint whipping cream

Stew the plums and orange juice gently until soft, then liquidise. Dissolve the sugar in water and boil for 2 minutes. Cool. Combine purée of plums and syrup, then freeze until the mushy stage. Whisk the egg whites in a very large bowl. Add fruit mixture while still whisking. Continue for 5 minutes, by which time the mixture will have filled the bowl. Lightly whip cream and fold into mixture. Place in a suitable container and freeze. Note the beautiful pink colour.

Flavouring: This is possible with other fruits, greengages, gooseberries, rhubarb and orange, but the colour is not always appetizing. With raspberries, strawberries, etc., there is no need to cook the fruit first; follow all the other instructions after having made a purée of the fruit.

Mrs. Richardson, Dalbeattie.

Ginger Trifle

8 trifle sponges
6 ozs ginger jam
6 ozs raspberries, fresh or frozen
¼ pint *Crabbie's* Green Ginger wine
4 eggs

1 oz caster sugar
Vanilla essence
¾ pint single cream
½ pint double cream

Split the trifle sponges and spread with jam. Place these in a trifle dish and sprinkle with raspberries on top. Pour over *Crabbie's* Green Ginger wine evenly and place dish on one side.

Separate 3 eggs, and whisk together 3 yolks, 1 whole egg, 1 oz caster sugar and a few drops of vanilla essence, until thick and creamy. Heat single cream until just below boiling point and pour over the egg mixture. Mix thoroughly. Pour this custard back into the pot and cook slowly over a low heat, stirring constantly. Do not boil. Pour the cooked custard mixture over the sponge and leave aside to cool. Whip double cream until stiff and pipe or spoon over the trifle. Decorate as required.

Stuart Barber, "L'Aperitif", Edinburgh.

Tiramiso

4 egg yolks
5 Tbsps sugar

1 pint cold, strong coffee
Chocolate powder

1 lb cream cheese	Cream
1½ pkts egg biscuits	Tia Maria, optional

Blend together the egg yolks, sugar and cheese. Layer a pudding dish with biscuits alternately dipped in the coffee then the egg mixture. Cover with chocolate powder, then cream, then chocolate powder again. Pour Tia Maria liqueur on top if desired.

Bertha Sinclair, Edinburgh.

Baked Bananas *- for the oven or barbeque, a most delicious pudding*

1 banana per person	1 tsp brandy per person, optional
1 oz plain chocolate per person	Whipped cream for serving

Oven temperature: 350°F. 175°C. Gas mark 4.

Put the bananas in their skins on a baking tray in a medium oven or over a barbeque. Leave until skins are black and bananas feel soft inside. They should be turned once during cooking. To serve, slit open in place, sprinkle chocolate inside skin and add brandy if used. Serve with whipped cream.

Anne Carter, St. Andrews.

Bananas with Coffee Cream *- serves 4*

Juice of 1 lemon	¼ pint whipped cream
4 large bananas, peeled and sliced	1 oz icing sugar
2 tsps instant coffee powder	1 oz walnut halves

Sprinkle lemon juice over bananas and divide into 4 individual glasses, reserving a few pieces for decoration. Dissolve coffee in a little hot water and stir into whipped cream. Fold in icing sugar and pile mixture on top of bananas. Decorate with banana slices and walnut halves.

Mairi Black, Rutherglen.

Banana Cream

2 ripe bananas
2 eggs, separated
¼ pint whipping cream

2 Tbsps sugar
Liqueur, optional
Cinnamon

Mash bananas and whisk egg whites until stiff. Whisk cream with sugar until stiff. Fold all three together and add liqueur if using, and sprinkle with cinnamon. Chill in glasses.

Mrs. E. Ormiston, Inverary.

Liqueured Peaches

4 peaches
½ pint water
4 ozs sugar

Thinly peeled lemon rind
2 Tbsps maraschino or orange
  liqueur

Put peaches in boiling water and remove the skin with a stainless steel knife, then cut in half to remove stones. Put water, sugar and lemon rind in a pan, dissolve sugar and bring to the boil. Add peaches and poach until softened. Drain carefully, reducing syrup to ⅓ of volume. Strain syrup and then stir in the liqueur. Pour over peaches and chill.

Wilma Aitken, Aberdeen.

Frosted Peaches

Swiss roll
1 tin peach halves
1 egg white

2 ozs caster sugar
Cherries for decoration

Oven temperature: 400°F. 205°C. Gas mark 6.

Soak Swiss roll slices in juice from peaches. Whisk egg white until stiff, then fold in the sugar. Place Swiss roll slices on a baking tray, cover with peach halves and top with meringue. Place in a hot oven for a few minutes to brown slightly, then decorate with cherries to serve.

Muriel Gilray, Edinburgh.

Watermelon Frappé - *very refreshing after a rich main course*

3 lb water melon
3 ozs caster sugar
Finely grated rind of ½ lemon

Finely grated rind and juice of
    1 large orange
1 Tbsp lemon juice

De-seed and peel the watermelon, then cut into cubes. Purée these cubes in batches in a blender or crush to a pulp with a potato masher until smooth. Put the sugar in a large bowl and add the orange and lemon rinds. Slowly stir in the orange and lemon juices and then the watermelon purée a little at a time, stirring constantly to dissolve the sugar. Pour the mixture into a suitable 2 pint container and freeze for about 3 hours until it is slushy. Turn the mixture into a large bowl and whisk to break up large ice crystals. Return to container, cover and freeze for a further 2 hours until frappé is firm. Serve in glass dishes or large glasses.

Rhoda Burdis, Brampton.

Meringue Surprise

Meringue nest
Fruit

Ice cream
Milk flake

Fill a meringue nest or shell with a spoonful of fruit, (oranges, cherries, etc.) Top with a scoopful of ice cream and sprinkle some crumbled milk flake over the nest.

Staff, Eastern General Hospital, Edinburgh.

Sanne's Pudding - *a Danish recipe*

2 eggs
3 tsps sugar
1 large pot natural yogurt

1 small pot cream
Vanilla essence

Whisk eggs and add the sugar, followed by yogurt then cream. Add vanilla essence to taste. Place in a fridge and serve very cold. This is a most refreshing summer dessert and should be served with crunchy broken rusks and/or summer fruit.

Sanne, Camphill Blair Drummond, as given to Anne Carter.

Creamy Yogurt Dessert

1 large whipping cream   Soft brown sugar
1 large plain yogurt

Whip the cream until very thick, fold in the yogurt and pour mixture into a wide based dish. Sprinkle soft brown sugar over surface quite thickly and leave to form crust in fridge overnight. Delicious on its own, or can be served with either chopped fruit in it, or with a fruit salad separately.

Mary Sandeman, T.V. Personality.

Happi's Raspberry Brulée

2 punnets of fresh or frozen   8 oz carton whipping or double
   raspberries   cream
1 Tbsp caster sugar   4 – 5 Tbsps demerara sugar

Put raspberries in a pyrex serving dish, whip cream and caster sugar and cover fruit entirely and smoothly. Sprinkle demerara sugar thickly and evenly over whole mixture and grill quickly for a few minutes until sugar bubbles, but not long enough for the cream to melt.

Moira Cousins, Glasgow.

Yogurt Dream - *serves 6 - 8*

1 lb or 500g carton fruit yogurt   10 oz carton whipping cream
   preferably tart, eg peach and
   redcurrant

Whip cream stiffly. Gently fold in yogurt.

Mairi Black, Rutherglen.

Lemon Mist

½ pint double cream   2 egg whites
3 lemons   Chopped nuts or coconut for

2 Tbsps caster sugar   decoration

Whip the cream until it holds its shape. Gradually fold in the lemon juice and sugar. Then add the stiffly beaten egg whites. Pile into four dishes and decorate with chopped nuts or coconut. Recommended to serve with sponge finger biscuits.

Kathleen Montgomery, Aberdeen and Muriel Gilray, Edinburgh.

Lemon Refrigerator Cake - *serves 8*

4 ozs butter   Grated rind and juice of 1 lemon
6 ozs caster sugar   8 small sponge cakes
3 eggs, separated   10 oz carton whipping cream

Cream butter and sugar until very white and fluffy. Beat in egg yolks and grated lemon rind and juice. Fold in stiffly beaten egg whites. Split sponge cakes into 2 or 3 layers and line an oblong tin approx 9 x 4 inches with alternate layers of sponge and lemon mixture, finishing with sponge. Cover and chill for 12 – 24 hours. Turn out onto a serving dish, cover with cream and decorate, either with angelica or lemon sweets. Serve with cream.

Audrey Cowan, Hamilton.

Swiss Cream - *serves 4 - 6*

4 ozs ratafia biscuits or sponge cake   2 ozs caster sugar
3 – 4 Tbsps sherry   ¼ – ½ pint double cream
1¼ ozs cornflour   2 tsps glacé cherries or nuts,
1 pint milk   chopped or grated
1 lemon

Put the ratafia biscuits or cake in the bottom of a dish and soak with sherry. Blend the cornflour with sufficient of the milk to make a smooth cream. Heat the remaining milk slowly with a thin strip of lemon. Strain onto the blended cornflour, return to the pan and cook thoroughly but gently for 3 – 4 minutes. Stir in the sugar and allow to cool. Whip the cream slightly and add this with the juice of the lemon, gently and gradually to the cool cornflour cream.

Re-sweeten if necessary. Pour over the soaked biscuits or cake and leave to cool. Decorate with chopped nuts or glacé cherries.

Kathleen Montgomery, Aberdeen.

Angels' Food

8 ozs marshmallows	2 small tins broken orange
½ pint whipping cream	segments, drained

Cut up the marshmallows into small pieces, either using scissors or melting them if preferred. Put these in a large bowl with orange segments and leave in fridge overnight. Whip cream until stiff and fold into mixture. Pile into individual glasses or one large bowl and decorate as desired.

Marjorie Macleod, Newcastle-under-Lyme.

Mousse

1 large tin evaporated milk   1 jelly, raspberry is recommended

Put evaporated milk to chill in the fridge for at least 2 hours. Make up the jelly using only 1 small cup of boiling water, then leave aside until nearly setting. Whisk milk to thicken and add to setting jelly. Whisk together until thick and fluffy – it makes a large bowlful. Allow to set.

Ena Barrie, Motherwell.

Chocolate Mousse

1 pint packet *Creamola* Chocolate	6 ozs plain chocolate
Pudding	1 lemon jelly
1 pint milk	Double cream, whipped

Make chocolate pudding with milk and add melted chocolate. Make up lemon jelly with only ½ pint water and when almost set add to chocolate pudding and whisk vigorously. Pour into a serving dish and when firm decorate with double cream.

Audrey Cowan, Hamilton.

Chocolate Brandy Whip

4 ozs milk chocolate
3 large eggs, separated
1 Tbsp hot water

½ oz butter
1 drop brandy essence
1 Tbsp caster sugar

Melt chocolate in a bowl and add the egg yolks one at a time. Beat well until stiff and creamy. Add hot water, butter in small pieces and finally essence. Whisk egg whites until stiff. Fold in sugar and then fold in chocolate mixture into beaten egg whites. Divide into individual sundae glasses and decorate with cream.

Eileen Dunn, Rutherglen.

Coffee Cream

7 ozs butter
1 oz plain flour
¼ pint milk ·
4 tsps instant coffee powder
6 ozs caster sugar

1 packet sponge fingers
4 Tbsps sherry
2 Tbsps water
Whipped cream and grated
   chocolate for decoration

Slowly melt 1 oz of butter in a small pan, stir in the flour and cook for 1 minute. Remove from heat and gradually add the milk and coffee powder. Replace pan on heat and bring to boil, stirring all the time. Cook gently for 2 minutes, then cool.

Cream together sugar and remaining butter. Add the cooled coffee sauce, a spoonful at a time and beat well. Mix sherry and water in a bowl. Put a layer of coffee cream into a glass serving dish. Lightly dip sponge fingers into sherry mixture and arrange in glass dish on top of the coffee cream. Repeat these 2 layers and finish with a layer of coffee mixture. Decorate with whipped cream and grated chocolate. Delicious served with fresh fruit.

Marjorie Macleod, Newcastle-under-Lyme.

Ambrosia Mould

3 ozs cornflour
2 pints milk

4 ozs sugar
¼ pint sherry

2 ozs butter   Wine sauce for serving

Blend cornflour with a little of the milk to a thin cream. Boil remainder of the milk with the butter, pour over blended cornflour, return to pan and cook thoroughly. Add sugar and sherry. Pour into a mould and turn out when cold, after 2 hours. Serve with wine sauce.

Mrs. Montgomery.

Baked Alaska

3 egg whites   Family pack of ice cream
Pinch of cream of tartar   8 inch sponge flan
3 level Tbsps caster sugar

Oven temperature: 430°F. 220°C. Gas mark 7.

Beat egg whites with cream of tartar until stiff. Beat in sugar. Quickly put ice cream on the centre of sponge, leaving a margin of cake showing all around the edge. Quickly cover ice cream and sponge with meringue. Put in oven for 3 – 5 minutes until meringue is lightly browned. Serve immediately.

Muriel Gilray, Edinburgh.

BAKING

Happy Home Recipe

4 cups love	3 cups forgiveness
2 cups loyalty	1 cup friendship
4 quarts faith	5 spoons hope
2 spoons tenderness	1 barrel laughter

Take love and loyalty. Mix thoroughly with faith. Blend with tenderness, kindness and understanding. Add friendship and hope. Sprinkle abundantly with laughter. Bake with sunshine. Serve daily in generous helpings.

Oatcakes

12 ozs medium oatmeal	2 Tbsps S.R. flour
1 tsp salt	½ tsp baking powder
2 ozs melted dripping	Hot water to mix

Oven temperature: 350°F. 175°C. Gas mark 4.

Mix all ingredients to a manageable consistency for rolling out. Take about a tennis ball's worth and roll out to a circle ¼ inch thick and cut into 4. Place on baking trays and bake in the top of the oven until light brown. This will make at least 2 dozen cakes.

David Ballingall, Bridge of Allan.

Apple or Banana Scones

8 ozs S.R. flour	Milk to mix
2 ozs margarine	1 apple, grated, or
2 ozs sugar	1 banana, mashed
1 egg, beaten	

Oven temperature: 430°F. 220°C. Gas mark 7.

Mix all ingredients together with enough milk to make a soft dough. Bake in oven until brown.

Sarah Scott, Broughty Ferry.

Apple Buns

2 medium cooking apples	1 tsp baking powder
8 ozs 100% wholemeal flour	6 ozs butter or margarine
Pinch of salt	2 ozs brown sugar
½ tsp cinnamon	1 egg, beaten

Oven temperature: 370°F. 190°C. Gas mark 5.

Core and dice the apples. Mix together the flour, salt, spice and baking powder in a basin, then rub in the butter until it is like fine breadcrumbs. Add remaining ingredients, including apples, and mix well. Place a heaped spoonful on a lightly greased baking tray and bake for 20 – 25 minutes until golden. Cool slightly before transferring to a wire tray.

Jean Inglis, Edinburgh.

Marmalade Scone Rings *- makes 8*

12 ozs S.R. flour	1 egg
Pinch of salt	7 Tbsps milk
2 ozs margarine	3 heaped Tbsps marmalade
1 oz caster sugar	2 ozs currants
Grated rind of 1 orange	1 oz melted butter

Oven temperature: 430°F. 220°C. Gas mark 7.

Pre-heat oven and brush a 7½ inch sandwich tin with cooking oil. Sieve flour and salt, then rub in the margarine. Stir in the sugar and orange rind. Beat together the egg and milk and add to the dry ingredients, mixing to a soft scone-like dough. Knead dough lightly and roll to about 9 x 12 inches. Spread surface with marmalade, sprinkle with currants and roll up starting with a long side. Cut roll into 8 equal slices and lay them in the tin with one in centre and the rest around the sides, cut sides upwards. Bake in a hot oven for about 20 minutes then brush melted butter over the tops. Cool on a wire tray. If you can serve the scones freshly baked, each piece pulls away separately.

To freeze: Marmalade scone rings freeze very well. Heat from frozen for 10 minutes in a moderate oven.

Mairi Black, Rutherglen.

Selkirk Bannocks - *Makes 2 large bannocks, enough for 8 portions*

2 ozs polyunsaturated margarine
¼ pint skimmed milk
2 tsps dried yeast

2 ozs soft brown sugar
8 ozs plain flour
4 ozs sultanas

Oven temperature: 430°F. 220°C. Gas mark 7.
Reducing to: 370°F. 190°C. Gas mark 5.

Warm the margarine and milk to body heat in a small pan, then pour onto yeast in a small bowl. Stir in 1 tsp of the sugar and leave in a warm place until frothy, about 10 minutes. Sieve the flour into a warmed bowl and stir in the remaining sugar and sultanas. Add the liquid and knead the dough for 5 minutes. Leave to rise, covered with a damp cloth or polythene, in a warm place until doubled in size, about 1 hour. Knead the dough again and divide it into two. Shape each piece into a circle and put on an oiled baking tray. Leave them to rise again in a warm place for about 20 minutes. Pre-heat the oven, then bake for about 15 minutes, reducing to lower heat for a further 15 – 20 minutes. Test by tapping the base, which should sound hollow. Cool the bannocks on a wire tray.

Rt. Hon. David Steel, M.P.

Bran Loaf

2 cups *All Bran*
2 cups milk
2 cups mixed dried fruit
2 cups soft brown sugar

2 eggs, beaten
2 cups S.R. flour
1 tsp spice

Oven temperature: 370°F. 190°C. Gas mark 5.

Soak together the bran, milk, fruit and sugar for 1 hour. Add the eggs, flour and spice, stir the mixture and divide into 3 well greased 1 lb loaf tins. Bake for approximately ¾ hour until firm. Turn out and allow to cool on a wire tray.
The mixture alternatively makes 2 larger 1 lb loaves, taking about 1 hour in the oven.

Mairi Black, Rutherglen.

Cheese Loaf

8 ozs S.R. flour
2 ozs margarine
3 ozs cheese, grated

1 cup milk
½ level tsp salt
Shake of pepper

Oven temperature: 400°F. 205°C. Gas mark 6.

Grease a 1 lb loaf tin. Mix flour and seasoning, then rub in the margarine. Stir cheese into mixture. Mix with milk to a soft but not sticky dough. Press into loaf tin then bake for 45 minutes. When cold, cut into 12 slices and sandwich together with butter or pickle.

Mairi Black, Rutherglen.

Orange or Lemon Loaf

2 ozs soft margarine
6 ozs sugar
1 egg
2 Tbsps milk

Grated rind and juice of 1 lemon
Grated rind and juice of 1 orange
7 ozs S.R. flour

Oven temperature: 350°F. 175°C. Gas mark 4.

Cream together the margarine and sugar, then add the egg, milk, juice and rind of lemon and orange. Finally fold in the flour. Bake in a lined 2 lb loaf tin for 50 – 60 minutes.

Audrey Cowan, Hamilton.

Banana Loaf

8 ozs S.R. flour
½ tsp salt
2 ozs margarine
2 eggs, beaten

2 level tsps baking powder
2 bananas, mashed
5 ozs sugar

Oven temperature: 450°F. 235°C. Gas mark 8.
Reducing to: 350°F. 175°C. Gas mark 4.

Grease a 1 lb loaf tin. Sieve flour, salt and baking powder together. Cream margarine and sugar, then beat in the eggs. Add flour and banana alternately and beat until smooth. Bake in the loaf tin for 1 hour. When putting loaf in oven, turn heat down to lower setting. Test with skewer. Allow to cool for a few minutes before taking out of tin.

Lockhart McEwan, Rutherglen.

Sultana Loaf

4 ozs margarine
1 cup sugar
2 cups sultanas
1 cup water

1 tsp bicarbonate of soda
2 large eggs, beaten
8 ozs S.R. flour

Oven temperature: 370°F. 190°C. Gas mark 5.

Simmer together for 15 minutes the margarine, sugar, sultanas, water and bicarbonate of soda. Cool this mixture and add the eggs and flour, then beat well. Line the bottom of a 2 lb loaf tin and grease well. Bake for 45 – 60 minutes. Test with skewer and leave in the tin until cool. Turn onto a wire tray.

Jean Simpson, Grangemouth.

Walnut Bread

1 oz yeast
⅓ pint water
4 ozs buttermilk
2 tsps salt

8 ozs 85% flour
12 ozs plain flour
2 ozs walnuts, chopped

Oven temperature: 430°F. 220°C. Gas mark 7.

Dissolve yeast in the water then add the buttermilk. Mix the dry ingredients together and add the liquid. Knead and leave to raise for about 30 minutes. Knead again and mould to a bread, put on a greased tray and leave to prove until double in size. Bake for about 30 minutes.

Lisbeth Nielsen (Denmark), Camphill Blair Drummond.

Tea Brack - *makes 2 loaves*

1 lb mixed dried fruit
8 ozs sugar
½ pint warm tea

1 egg, beaten
2 rounded Tbsps marmalade
1 lb S.R. flour

Oven temperature: 330°F. 165°C. Gas mark 3.

Grease 2 x 1 lb loaf tins. Put fruit, sugar and tea in a bowl and stir until sugar is melted. Stir in egg and marmalade. Add flour and mix well, then pour into tins. Bake in the centre of oven for 1¾ hours until well cooked. Test with skewer. Leave in tin for 10 minutes. These loaves can be frozen, or stored for upto 4 weeks in an airtight tin.

Mairi Black, Rutherglen.

Old Fashioned Nut Loaf

5 ozs butter or margarine
6 ozs sugar
2 eggs
4 ozs chopped nuts

9 ozs S.R. flour
Milk to mix
Nuts to decorate

Oven temperature: 350°F. 175°C. Gas mark 4.

Line a loaf tin. Cream fat and sugar together until light. Beat in eggs and add chopped nuts. Sieve flour, add alternately with a little milk to make a soft consistency. Put mixture in tin and place halved nuts on top. Bake for 1¼ hours.

Muriel Gilray, Edinburgh.

Treacle Loaf

2 ozs margarine
3 ozs sugar
1 Tbsp treacle
½ cup boiling water

8 ozs S.R. flour
1 tsp ground ginger
1 tsp mixed spices
½ tsp baking powder

Oven temperature: 330°F. 165°C. Gas mark 3.

Put margarine, sugar and treacle in a pan to melt. Add hot water, then add all dry ingredients. Put into loaf tin and bake for ¾ hour.

Mairi Black, Rutherglen.

Nut and Raisin Bread

2 ozs lard or margarine	2 ozs sultanas
12 ozs wholemeal flour	4 ozs chopped nuts
¼ tsp salt	1 egg
2 tsps baking powder	½ pint milk
2 ozs sugar	

Oven temperature: 400°F. 205°C. Gas mark 6.

Rub the fat into the sifted flour and salt. Add remaining dry ingredients and mix to a fairly soft dough with the egg and milk. Put into a well greased tin and bake in a fairly hot oven for about 1 hour.

Kathleen Montgomery, Aberdeen and Lockhart McEwan, Rutherglen.

Date Loaf

2 ozs margarine	8 ozs dates
¾ cup caster sugar	1 tsp bicarbonate of soda
1 egg, beaten	¾ cup boiling water
1¾ cups flour	2 ozs walnuts, optional
1 tsp vanilla essence	

Oven temperature: 350°F. 175°C. Gas mark 4.

Cream the margarine and sugar. Add the well beaten egg and flour alternately, then add vanilla essence, chopped dates and sprinkle bicarbonate of soda over the top of them. Cover with boiling water and mix well together. Lastly add chopped nuts.

Audrey Cowan, Hamilton.

Christmas Fruit Loaf

½ oz fresh yeast or 2 tsps dried yeast	4 ozs softened butter
3½ fl ozs lukewarm milk	½ tsp cinnamon
½ tsp sugar	2 tsps vanilla essence
1 lb wheatmeal flour	Grated rind of 1 lemon
Pinch of salt	8 ozs mixed candied fruits
2 ozs brown sugar	2 eggs, beaten

Oven temperature: 350°F. 175°C. Gas mark 4.

Mix yeast with milk, and if using dried yeast, add white sugar and leave until frothy, 10 – 15 minutes. Mix flour, salt and brown sugar, rubbing in the butter. Add yeast liquid and remaining ingredients. Mix to a soft dough then knead for 10 minutes. Cover and leave until doubled in bulk in a warm place. Punch down, form into a loaf shape and place in a greased 2 lb tin. Cover and leave in a warm place for 30 minutes until dough has reached the top of tin. Bake for 45 minutes, then leave to cool before removing from tin.

Staff, Eastern General Hospital, Edinburgh.

Singin' Hinny – *an old Northumbrian recipe*

8 ozs plain flour	3 ozs lard
¼ level tsp of bicarbonate of soda	1 oz sugar, optional
½ level tsp salt	3 ozs currants
½ level tsp cream of tartar	7 Tbsps milk

Sieve the dry ingredients together and rub in the fat. Add currants and sugar then enough milk to mix to a soft dough. Turn out and knead lightly. Roll into a circle and cook on a moderately hot, well greased griddle or heavy frying pan for 10 – 15 minutes. Cool slightly and cut into sections. Cut open and butter hot or cold.

Betty Smeaton, Newcastle upon Tyne.

Blooming Bun

4 ozs S.R. flour	2 – 3 drops vanilla essence
Pinch of baking powder	Milk

2 ozs sugar
2 ozs margarine
1 egg

Handful of raisins
Icing
Chopped nuts and cherries

Oven temperature: 430°F. 220°C. Gas mark 7.

Mix flour, baking powder and sugar, then rub in the margarine until it is like breadcrumbs. Add egg, essence, and sufficient milk to make a batter which is thicker than pancake batter. Add fruit. Bake for 20 minutes. Ice when cold and sprinkle with chopped nuts and cherries.

Staff, Eastern General Hospital, Edinburgh.

Auntie Kate's Gingerbread

4 ozs margarine
4 ozs sugar
2 Tbsps treacle
2 eggs
8 ozs plain flour

1 tsp mixed spice
1 tsp ginger
1 tsp bicarbonate of soda
½ cup boiling water

Oven temperature: 370°F. 190°C. Gas mark 5.

Cream margarine and sugar, then add the treacle gradually with the eggs. Mix in the flour and spices, leaving bicarbonate of soda dissolved in the boiling water until last. Place in a lined loaf tin and bake for ¾ – 1 hour.

Jean Simpson, Grangemouth.

Apple Tartlets

Shortcrust pastry
2 ozs margarine
2 ozs sugar

1 egg, beaten
1 large apple, grated

Oven temperature: 400°F. 205°C. Gas mark 6.

Make shortcrust pastry cases. Mix together other ingredients and fill cases, then bake in a hot oven until slightly brown.

Sarah Scott, Broughty Ferry.

Swiss Tarts - *makes 18*

8 ozs margarine
2 ozs caster sugar
Vanilla essence

8 ozs plain flour
Icing sugar
Jam

Oven temperature: 370°F. 190°C. Gas mark 5.

Cream margarine and sugar, add essence and 4 ozs of flour, beating well. Add remaining flour and beat again. Pipe mixture into paper cases. Start from the centre and use a spiral movement, leaving a shallow depression in the middle. Bake for 15 – 20 minutes, taking care tops do not become brown. When cool dust with icing sugar and fill hollows with jam.

Mairi Black, Rutherglen.

Coconut Fingers

3 ozs margarine
6 ozs plain flour
2 ozs sugar
2 large eggs, separated

½ tsp almond essence
4 Tbsps jam
Coconut

Oven temperature: 350°F. 175°C. Gas mark 4.

Rub margarine into flour until mixture resembles crumbs. Stir in sugar, egg yolks and essence until the ingredients bind together to form a paste. On a lightly floured working surface, knead the paste lightly until smooth, then roll it out to fit the base of tin. Spread jam over pastry.
To make the meringue topping, whisk the egg whites until stiff, and using a metal spoon fold in extra sugar, flour and coconut, then spread this mixture over the jam base. Bake for 30 minutes and allow to cool before cutting.

Muriel Gilray, Edinburgh.

Marzipan Slices

5 ozs digestive biscuits, crushed
Almond essence

Marzipan
4 ozs cooking chocolate

3 ozs margarine   Flaked almonds
Jam

Mix biscuits and a few drops of almond essence in melted margarine, then press into a Swiss roll tin. Leave to set. Cover with a layer of jam then a thin layer of marzipan. Spread with melted chocolate on top and sprinkle with flaked almonds. When cool cut into slices or squares.

Pat Scott, Edinburgh.

Edinburgh Snowballs

1 cup white sugar   2 ozs chopped walnuts
2 ozs butter   2 cups rice crispies
4 ozs chopped dates   Coconut
1 egg

Blend the sugar, butter, dates and egg for 10 minutes over a low heat. Take off, cool and add chopped nuts and rice crispies. When quite cool, roll into balls, approximately 25 in number. Coat with coconut. Keep in fridge. May be kept in freezer until required.

Edith McDougall, Edinburgh.

Nutty Squares

4 ozs butter   3 ozs sultanas
5 ozs demerara sugar   3 ozs chopped walnuts
2 eggs   6 ozs S.R. flour
½ tsp vanilla essence   Icing sugar
3 ozs desiccated coconut

Oven temperature: 350°F. 175°C. Gas mark 4.

Grease a Swiss roll tin. Cream butter and sugar, then add eggs one at a time, beating well. Mix in vanilla, coconut, sultanas and nuts. Fold in sifted flour. Spread in tin and bake for 45 minutes. Cool and cut into squares. Dust with icing sugar.

Pat Scott, Edinburgh.

Ginger Fudge Squares

2 ozs margarine
4 ozs soft brown sugar
1 Tbsp syrup
1 small tin condensed milk

8 ozs crushed ginger snaps
1 small tsp ground ginger
Chocolate, melted

Mix together the margarine, sugar, syrup and milk over a low heat. Add the ginger snaps and the ground ginger, stirring well. Put mixture into a Swiss roll tin and cover with a thin layer of chocolate.

Marjorie Macleod, Newcastle–under–Lyme.

Alternative finish: Ice with lemon icing, made with 8 ozs icing sugar and sufficient lemon juice to bind. Add yellow colouring if desired.

Mairi Black, Rutherglen.

Peanut Crunch

1 cup syrup
1 cup brown sugar
1 cup peanut butter

2 good cups rice crispies
2 good cups cornflakes

Melt syrup and sugar in a saucepan. Add peanut butter. Pour over crispies and cornflakes in a bowl and mix well. Press into a Swiss roll tin, cutting when set.

Edith McDougall, Edinburgh.

Paradise Cake

For the base:
5 ozs plain flour
4 ozs butter

1 oz sugar
1 egg yolk

For the filling:
4 ozs margarine
1 egg

1 cup sultanas and currants
2 Tbsps glacé cherries, chopped
2 Tbsps chopped walnuts

1 egg white

5 ozs caster sugar

2 Tbsps ground almonds

2 Tbsps ground rice

Oven temperature: 350°F. 175°C. Gas mark 4.

Grease a Swiss roll tin. To make the base, rub fat into flour, then add the sugar and egg yolk. Knead together and roll out to line tin. Crimp edges.
To make the filling, mix together the margarine, eggs and 4 ozs of caster sugar. Add remaining ingredients, except balance of caster sugar, and mix well, before spreading evenly onto the shortbread base. Bake for 30 – 35 minutes until firm. Sprinkle with sugar. Cut when cool and remove from tin.

Pat Scott, Edinburgh.

Chocolate Fudge Cake

5 ozs sugar

4 ozs margarine

1 small tin condensed milk

8 ozs digestive biscuits, crushed

Melted chocolate to cover

Put sugar, margarine and condensed milk in a medium pan and melt over low heat. Add crushed biscuits. Put in a shallow tin and press down. Cover with melted chocolate and when set, cut into small squares or slices.

Simon Carter, Camphill Blair Drummond.

Munchy Date Layer

8 ozs butter

4 ozs wholemeal flour

6 ozs rolled oats

8 ozs chopped dates

1 Tbsp lemon juice

Pinch of cinnamon

2 Tbsps water

1 Tbsp honey

Oven temperature: 350°F. 175°C. Gas mark 4.

Make crumbly pastry by rubbing the butter into flour and oat mixture. Press half of pastry into a greased tray. Mix all remaining ingredients to make the filling, spreading this over the pastry. Cover with remaining pastry. Bake for 20 – 25 minutes.

Sarah Scott, Broughty Ferry.

Lemon and Coconut Bake

Sweet shortcrust pastry   6 ozs coconut
1 small tin condensed milk   5 ozs lemon curd
1 egg

Oven temperature: 350°F. 175°C. Gas mark 4.

Line a flan tin with sweet shortcrust pastry. Mix remaining ingredients together and spread over the base. Bake in the oven for 30 – 35 minutes.

Sarah Scott, Edinburgh.

Coffee Bars

8 ozs digestive biscuits   7 ozs icing sugar
1 small tin condensed milk   3 ozs butter
2 Tbsps ground almonds   Chocolate
2 Tbsps coffee essence   Margarine

To make the base, crush the biscuits, then add condensed milk, almonds, coffee and 4 ozs of icing sugar, mixing well together. Spread this mixture onto a Swiss roll tin. To make the topping, cream together butter and remaining icing sugar and spread this over the base. Melt chocolate with margarine and pour over butter icing.

Edith McDougall, Edinburgh.

Date and Ginger Crunchies

4 ozs margarine   1 oz cherries, chopped
4 ozs caster sugar   4 ozs rice crispies
8 ozs dates, chopped   4 ozs chocolate
½ tsp ground ginger

Put margarine, sugar, dates and ginger in a large pan and melt to a paste. Remove from heat and stir in the cherries and rice crispies. Mix well and spread onto a Swiss roll tin. Cover with melted chocolate.

Pat Scott, Edinburgh.

Chocolate Fudge Tart

Sweet shortcrust pastry
4 ozs margarine
4 ozs caster sugar

6 ozs dried milk
1½ ozs cocoa
6 ozs dried fruit

Oven temperature: 350°F. 175°C. Gas mark 4.

Line a flan case with sweet shortcrust pastry. Cream together the margarine and sugar, then mix in dried milk, cocoa and fruit with enough boiling water to make it spreadable over the pastry. Press into flan case, then sprinkle with a little sugar, before baking for 20 minutes. Cut while hot.

Sarah Scott, Broughty Ferry.

Picnic Slices

8 ozs cooking chocolate, milk
2 ozs butter
4 ozs caster sugar
1 egg, beaten

4 ozs coconut
2 ozs sultanas
2 ozs glacé cherries, chopped

Oven temperature: 310°F. 155°C. Gas mark 2.

Break chocolate into pieces and melt in a bowl over a pan of hot water. Pour into a greased Swiss roll tin. Cream butter and sugar, then add all remaining ingredients, mixing well. Spread over the chocolate. Bake for 45 minutes and mark into slices 5 minutes later. Leave in the tin until cold.

Lockhart McEwan, Rutherglen.

Toffee Crisps

4 ozs margarine
4 ozs marshmallows

4 ozs cream toffee
1 small packet rice crispies

Melt together the margarine, marshmallows and toffee in a pan, then add the rice crispies. Press mixture into a greased baking tray, and when cool, cut into squares.

Lockhart McEwan, Rutherglen.

Canadian Flan

4 ozs short crust pastry
1 cup brown sugar
½ cup desiccated coconut
½ cup walnuts
1 cup mixed fruit

¼ tsp baking powder
2 Tbsps S.R. flour
1 egg, beaten
Jam

Oven temperature: 400°F. 205°C. Gas mark 6.

Line a greased Swiss roll tin with the pastry. Mix all dry ingredients together and bind with the egg. Spread pastry with jam and then with filling. Bake for 20 minutes.

Lockhart McEwan, Rutherglen.

Mincemeat and Walnut Whirls

1 packet frozen puff pastry
Mincemeat

Chopped walnuts

Oven temperature: 430°F. 220°C. Gas mark 7.

Thaw the pastry and roll out to a rectangle 10 inches wide; the length will depend on quantity used. Spread a layer of mincemeat over the pastry to within 1 inch of one long side. Sprinkle on some chopped walnuts. Damp the 1 inch edge of pastry. Roll up starting on the long side opposite the damp strip. Seal well on the damp edge keeping the join underneath. Cut into ½ inch slices. Place each slice flat onto a greased baking tray, and bake for 15 minutes. Remove from tray turning underside uppermost.

Mairi Black, Rutherglen.

Chocolate, Date and Cherry Crispies

4 ozs butter
4 ozs sugar
6 ozs chopped dates

2 ozs glacé cherries
4 ozs plain chocolate
3 ozs rice crispies

Gently melt butter and sugar in a large pan. Add chopped dates, cherries and plain chocolate. Stir well over a low heat until chocolate melts, then stir in rice crispies. Turn into a shallow tin, put in fridge for 2 hours then cut into slices. To finish, may be covered in chocolate.

Miss. S. Carter.

Brunch

1 cup S.R. flour
1 cup cornflakes
1 cup porage oats
1 cup coconut

½ cup sugar
5 ozs margarine
Icing sugar and hot water

Oven temperature: 450°F. 235°C. Gas mark 8.

Grease a Swiss roll tin. Mix dry ingredients together, except for icing sugar. Melt the margarine and mix into dry ingredients, then press mixture into the Swiss roll tin. Bake for about 20 minutes until golden brown. Ice the cake while still hot in the tin. Leave to cool and for the icing to set, then cut into fingers before removing from tin.

Mairi Black, Rutherglen.

Alternatively, with this recipe, use a chocolate or lemon icing.

Lockhart McEwan.

Wonder Bites

2 ozs butter
4 ozs icing sugar
2 ozs chopped walnuts
3 ozs cherries, chopped

1 tsp coffee essence
3 ozs desiccated coconut
6 ozs cooking chocolate

Cream the butter and sugar. Add all the remaining ingredients, except chocolate, and roll into small balls. Put into fridge to firm while melting chocolate. Coat with chocolate and place on greaseproof paper.

Pat Scott, Edinburgh.

Marshmallow Balls

2 ozs margarine
2 Tbsps milk
5 Tbsps coconut
1 cup porridge oats
2 Tbsps drinking chocolate powder

3 Tbsps sugar
Vanilla essence
20 – 24 marshmallows
Chocolate vermicelli

Melt margarine with the milk in a pan. Stir in the dry ingredients and vanilla essence. When cool, cover marshmallows with mixture and toss in a paper bag with vermicelli.

Mhairi Black, Camphill Blair Drummond.

Praline Bar

4 ozs soft margarine
2 Tbsps caster sugar
2 Tbsps golden syrup
Handful of raisins

12 ozs shortcake biscuits
½ level Tbsp cocoa plus 6 ozs plain
    cooking chocolate, or
10 ozs chocolate

Melt margarine, sugar and syrup in a large saucepan. Add cocoa and raisins. Remove from heat. Break biscuits into very small pieces and add to mixture in pan, then mix thoroughly. Spread in a Swiss roll tin and press down until smooth. Pour melted chocolate over top. Allow to harden before cutting into 24 squares.

Audrey Cowan, Hamilton.

Florentines - makes 12 - 24

4 ozs butter
4 ozs caster sugar
2 ozs glacé cherries, finely chopped
4 ozs peel, finely chopped

4 ozs blanched almonds, finely
    chopped
1 oz flaked almonds
2 Tbsps whipped cream
4 ozs plain chocolate

Oven temperature: 370°F. 190°C. Gas mark 5.

Melt butter and sugar together over a low heat, stirring all the time. Bring slowly to the boil and stir in fruit, nuts and finally cream. Stir well and allow to cool. Spoon onto trays allowing space to spread. Bake for 7 – 10 minutes until flat and golden. Leave until nearly cold then lift carefully. Spread with melted chocolate and just before setting, mark wavy lines with fork.

Mairi Black, Rutherglen.

Florencia Fingers

3 ozs margarine
2 level Tbsps syrup
4 ozs muesli
1 oz demerara sugar

1 oz chopped peel
1 oz glacé cherries, chopped
2 ozs plain cooking chocolate

Oven temperature: 350°F. 175°C. Gas mark 4.

Grease a tin with melted fat and line base with greaseproof paper. Melt the margarine and syrup in a saucepan over a low heat. Stir in the muesli, sugar, peel and cherries. When thoroughly combined, turn mixture into tin and press level with a spoon. Cook in the centre of oven for 20 – 30 minutes until golden brown. Leave to cool in tin. Melt chocolate and spread on top.

Muriel Gilray, Edinburgh.

Sherry Truffles

4 ozs fresh butter or unsalted
  margarine
4 ozs coconut, sponge cake or
  biscuits
4 ozs icing sugar
4 ozs drinking chocolate powder

1 Tbsp sherry
Some chopped nuts, raisins,
  ginger, cherries, etc. Anything
  you fancy.
Vermicelli

Mix ingredients together, roll into balls then toss in vermicelli. Put in fridge overnight.

Mairi Black, Rutherglen.

Chocolate Butter Crunchies

1 packet small sponge fingers   ¼ tsp vanilla essence
3 ozs butter   4 ozs cooking chocolate

Dice sponge finger biscuits then fry in melted butter until crisp. Cool. Melt chocolate and add vanilla essence and fried cubes. Spoon into small cake cases.

Eileen Dunn, Rutherglen.

Lemon Cake

4 ozs margarine   2 egg, beaten
4 ozs sugar   Juice of 1 lemon
4 ozs S.R. flour   5 ozs caster sugar

Oven temperature: 350°F. 175°C. Gas mark 4.

Melt the margarine and pour over the sugar. Mix in the beaten eggs and flour alternately. Place in a greased tin and bake for 30 minutes.
To make the topping, blend the lemon juice and caster sugar, then pour this over the cake while still hot, to make a crisp, tangy topping.

Pat Scott, Edinburgh.

Carrot Cake

3 cups grated carrots   ½ tsp nutmeg
1½ cups brown sugar   1 tsp cinnamon
1 cup wholemeal flour   ½ cup sultanas or ½ cup coconut,
1 cup S.R. flour   optional
3 eggs   Small packet of soft cheese
1 cup oil   Icing sugar
½ tsp baking powder

Oven temperature: 350°F. 175°C. Gas mark 4.

Mix together all ingredients except cheese and icing sugar. Fill a 7 inch square baking tin and cook for 1 hour.

To make the topping, mix the cheese with icing sugar.

C. Robbie.

Dorset Apple Cake

4 ozs margarine
Pinch of salt
8 ozs flour, white or wholemeal
1½ tsps baking powder
Sugar to taste

8 ozs apples, peeled, cored and
chopped
1 egg or 3 Tbsps milk
2 Tbsps currants or raisins, optional

Oven temperature: 350°F. 175°C. Gas mark 4.

Grease a round flat tin. Rub margarine into salt and flour, then add baking powder. Mix sugar and apples together and add to flour mixture. Add currants or raisins if liked. Add egg or milk to make a firm dough. Put mixture in the tin 1 inch thick, and bake in the oven for 45 – 60 minutes.

Betty Smeaton, Newcastle upon Tyne.

Fatless Sponge

3 eggs
3 ozs granulated sugar
3 ozs S.R. flour

Cream or jam for filling
Icing sugar for topping

Oven temperature: 400°F. 205°C. Gas mark 6.

Whisk together the eggs and sugar until very light. Fold in the sifted flour. Divide mixture into 2 round sandwich tins and bake in the oven for about 10 minutes. Cool on a wire tray, then sandwich with cream or jam. Sieve icing sugar over the top.

Mary Sandeman, T.V. Personality.

Black Forest Gâteau

4 eggs
4 ozs caster sugar

Whipped cream and cherry jam for
filling

3 ozs S.R. flour
½ level tsp baking powder
1 oz cocoa
2 ozs butter, melted

Whipped cream, vermicelli,
    chocolate flake and cherries for
    topping

Oven temperature: 350°F. 175°C. Gas mark 4.

Whisk eggs and sugar until double in bulk. Using a metal spoon, fold in the flour, baking powder and cocoa. Add melted butter. Bake in 2 x 8 inch tins until spongy to the touch. Turn out onto wire trays to cool. Sandwich together with whipped cream and cherry jam. Decorate with cream, vermicelli, chocolate flake and cherries.

Eileen Dunn, Rutherglen.

Pineapple Cake

7 ozs S.R. flour
5 ozs caster sugar
3 ozs luxury margarine
4 ozs tinned pineapple pieces

2 eggs
¼ tsp salt
A few pineapple pieces and cream
    for filling

Oven temperature: 370°F. 190°C. Gas mark 5.

Put flour and sugar in a bowl. Put margarine, pineapple, eggs and salt in a liquidiser and blend until smooth. Combine these with dry ingredients and pour into greased sandwich tins, baking for 25 minutes. Cool. For the filling, blend the cream in a liquidiser until thick. Fold in well drained pineapple pieces. Sandwich cakes together with mixture.

Kathleen Montgomery, Aberdeen.

Chocolate and Orange Cake

8 ozs margarine
8 ozs sugar
4 eggs
8 ozs flour
1 heaped tsp baking powder

Grated rind of 1 orange
2 Tbsps cocoa
5 Tbsps milk
For icing, orange juice, icing sugar
    and cocoa

Oven temperature: 330°F. 165°C. Gas mark 3.

Cream the margarine and sugar, then add the eggs, flour and baking powder, orange rind, cocoa and milk. Fill a greased loaf tin and bake for about 45 minutes. When cold, cover with icing, made from mixture of orange juice, icing sugar and cocoa.

Lisbeth Nielsen (Denmark), Camphill Blair Drummond.

Chilled Crabbie's and Chocolate Cake

4 ozs plain chocolate	1 Tbsp *Crabbie's* Green Ginger
2 ozs butter	wine
1 egg	2 ozs crystallized ginger, roughly
3 ozs gingernut biscuits	chopped
	Icing sugar

Melt plain chocolate gently in a bowl over a pan of hot water. Melt butter separately over a low heat. Whisk egg until frothy, then whisk in melted chocolate and butter. Put gingernut biscuits into a cloth and crush with a rolling pin. Stir the crushed biscuits into the chocolate mix along with wine and crystallized ginger. Pour the mixture into a small shallow cake tin or dish and leave in the fridge for at least one hour to set. Serve dusted with icing sugar.

Stuart Barber, "L'Aperitif", Edinburgh.

Courting Cake - *an old Cumberland Recipe*

10 ozs S.R. flour, plain or	2 eggs, beaten
wholemeal	Raspberry jam
4 ozs sugar	Icing or butter cream for top,
4 ozs butter or margarine	optional

Oven temperature: 350°F. 175°C. Gas mark 4.

Mix the flour and sugar, then rub in the fat. Add eggs and knead to a paste. Cut mixture in two and roll half to fit a Swiss roll tin. Spread with Raspberry jam and cover with other half of mixture. Prick well and bake for 35 minutes. Cover with icing or butter cream if desired.

Betty Smeaton, Newcastle upon Tyne.

Yum Yum Cake -*this cake almost melts in the mouth!*

2 ozs brown sugar
2 ozs margarine
2 eggs yolks, beaten
6 ozs S.R. flour
1 tsp vanilla essence

For the topping:
2 egg whites
4 ozs caster sugar
1 oz chopped walnuts
1 oz cherries, chopped

Oven temperature: 350°F. 175°C. Gas mark 4.

Cream the sugar and margarine until light and fluffy. Add the egg yolks and flour and finally the vanilla essence. Mix together by hand to a stiff paste and place in a greased swiss roll tin.
To make the topping, beat the egg whites until stiff and gradually blend in the sugar, nuts and cherries. Spread evenly over the base and bake in the oven for 20 – 30 minutes until nicely browned.

Edith McDougall, Edinburgh.

Carrot and Apple Cake

2 cups wholewheat flour
1 level tsp baking powder
1 level tsp bicarbonate of soda
1 cup raw sugar, or mix of sugar,
  honey and molasses

2 eggs
Pinch of salt
1 tsp mixed spice
1 cup grated carrot and apple
⅓ pint vegetable oil

Oven temperature: 370°F. 190°C. Gas mark 5.

Mix all ingredients together until dropping consistency, adding extra milk if necessary. Pour into greased loaf tin and bake for at least 45 minutes.

Jean Inglis, Edinburgh.

Brunsvigere - *a Danish Birthday Cake*

2 ozs butter
⅓ pint milk
1 oz fresh yeast
1 oz sugar

For the topping:
4 ozs butter
4 ozs dark brown sugar
2 Tbsps syrup

½ tsp salt
12 ozs plain flour

Oven temperature: 400°F. 205°C. Gas mark 6.

Melt the butter in a pan and add the milk. When lukewarm, stir in the fresh yeast. Add remaining base ingredients and mix well, then leave to rise for 30 minutes. For the topping, heat all ingredients together until boiling, then cool. Roll dough and place in a baking tray, then pour topping mixture over. Leave to rise for 20 minutes. Bake for 15 minutes.

Ukrainian Poppy Seed Cake

1 cup poppy seeds
1½ cups milk
8 ozs butter
1½ cups light brown sugar

3 eggs, separated
1¾ cups plain flour
2½ tsps baking powder
½ tsp salt
Juice of ½ lemon

Oven temperature: 350°F. 175°C. Gas mark 4.

Put poppy seeds and milk in a saucepan and heat only to boiling point. Remove from heat and leave to stand for 20 minutes. Cream butter and sugar until fluffy. Beat in the egg yolks, followed by flour, baking powder and salt. Mix well. Beat egg whites until stiff, but not dry. Fold into the butter mixture, and then fold in the poppy seeds and milk. Blend lightly together, then add lemon juice. Bake in a well greased loaf tin for 45 – 50 minutes, or a 9 inch square tin for 35 minutes. Test with skewer.

Rebecca Thomson, South America.

Cheap Fruit Cake

½ pint milk
2 ozs margarine
3 ozs sugar
1 teacup mixed fruit

1 Tbsp golden syrup
9 ozs S.R. flour
½ tsp bicarbonate of soda
1 tsp mixed spice

Oven temperature: 310°F. 155°C. Gas mark 2.

Place milk, margarine, sugar, fruit and syrup in a pan and simmer for 5 minutes. Leave to cool and then pour onto mixture of flour, soda and spice. Put in a loaf tin and bake for 1 hour.

Betty Smeaton, Newcastle upon Tyne.

Shearer's Cake

8 ozs butter or margarine
2 cups granulated sugar
2 cups water
1 lb mixed fruit

1 level tsp bicarbonate of soda
2 cups plain flour
2 cups S.R. flour

Oven temperature: 330°F. 165°C. Gas mark 3.

Put all ingredients except flour in a large pan. Bring to boil and boil for 3 minutes. Cool. Mix in flour, then mix all together smoothly. Bake for 1¼ – 1½ hours in a greased tin.

Ena Barrie, Motherwell.

Jill's Sour Cream Cinnamon Cake

2 cups sugar
1 cup margarine
2 eggs
1 cup soured cream
1 cup S.R. flour
1 cup plain flour

1 tsp baking powder
¼ tsp salt
3 tsps vanilla essence
1 tsp cinnamon
½ cup soft brown sugar
½ cup chopped nuts, any kind

Oven temperature: 350°F. 175°C. Gas mark 4.

Cream together the sugar and margarine. Add eggs and fold in the soured cream. Gradually add flour, baking powder, salt and 1 tsp of vanilla essence. Put half of this mixture in a greased and floured tin; one with the centre out. Mix remaining ingredients in a bowl and put half of this nut mixture onto the cake mixture in the tin. Cover with second half of cake mixture, and top with remaining nut mixture. Bake for 1 – 1¼ hours, or until ready, certainly not less than 1 hour. Carefully remove from tin and cool.

Moira Cousins, Glasgow.

The Queen Mother's Cake

1 breakfast cup boiling water
8 ozs chopped dates
1 tsp bicarbonate of soda
8 ozs sugar
3 ozs butter
1 egg, beaten

2 ozs chopped walnuts
10 ozs plain flour
1 tsp baking powder
1 tsp salt
1 tsp vanilla essence

For the topping:
5 Tbsps brown sugar
2 Tbsps butter

2 Tbsps cream
Chopped nuts

Oven temperature: 350°F. 175°C. Gas mark 4.

Pour boiling water over the chopped dates and bicarbonate of soda. Let it stand for the time it takes to mix together all the remaining base ingredients. Add this mixture to the dates, and place in a 9 x 12 inch tin. Bake for 35 minutes in the oven.

For the topping, mix together the sugar, butter and cream, then boil for three minutes. DO NOT let it boil for longer, as otherwise it will turn to toffee; it should have the consistency of fudge. Spread this mixture on the cake and sprinkle with chopped nuts.

Her Majesty, The Queen Mother.

This is the QUEEN MOTHER'S favourite cake recipe. At her request, it must not be GIVEN, but sold for 10 pence and the money donated to a charitable organization.

Plain Jumblies - *makes 40 biscuits*

3 ozs white cooking fat
2 ozs butter
6 ozs soft brown sugar

1 egg, beaten
8 ozs S.R. flour

Oven temperature: 370°F. 190°C. Gas mark 5.

Cream the fat and sugar until light and fluffy. Add the egg to the creamed mixture a little at a time, beating well after each addition. Stir in the flour with a knife until it forms a firm dough. Roll this mixture into small balls the size of a walnut, and place on a greased baking sheet, a little apart to allow for spreading. Press each lightly with a fork and bake for about 15 minutes.

Mrs. T. Carter.

Nutty Biscuits - *makes 30 biscuits*

8 ozs S.R. flour	2 ozs nuts, finely chopped
8 ozs soft brown sugar	1 egg
3 ozs instant creaming fat	Pinch of salt

Oven temperature: 370°F. 190°C. Gas mark 5.

Put all ingredients in a bowl and fork mix together for 1 minute. Leave in a cool place for 30 minutes. Shape into a long roll on a lightly sugared pastry board, then cut into ½ inch thick slices. Place rounds on greased baking trays spaced well apart. Bake for 15 – 20 minutes in the oven. Keep in an airtight tin.

Lockhart McEwan, Rutherglen.

Melting Moments

4 ozs margarine	5 ozs S.R. flour
2 ozs caster sugar	Vanilla essence
1 egg, beaten	Cornflakes

Oven temperature: 350°F. 175°C. Gas mark 4.

Cream the margarine and sugar. Alternately, add the beaten egg and sieved flour to the mixture. Add essence and beat until smooth. Roll a small teaspoon of the mixture in slightly crushed cornflakes. Place on baking trays and flatten slightly. Cook for 20 minutes.

Mairi Black, Rutherglen.

Anzacs - *Australian cookies*

6 ozs butter	4 ozs plain flour

1 tsp syrup
1 tsp bicarbonate of soda
2 Tbsps boiling water

2 cups rolled oats
6 ozs sugar
4 ozs raisins, chopped

Oven temperature: 310°F. 155°C. Gas mark 2.

Melt the butter and syrup. Dissolve the bicarbonate of soda in the boiling water and add to butter. Mix together the flour, oats, sugar and raisins then pour the liquid onto them. Mix well and place in teaspoonfuls on a greased tray, allowing room for spreading. Bake for 15 minutes. Cool on a wire tray.

Eva Hewertson, Kendal.

Oat Biscuits - *Danske Havregrynskager*

1 cup melted butter
2 cups oatflakes
1 cup flour
1 egg, beaten

1½ cups sugar
1 tsp ammonium carbonate
   – can be purchased in a chemist

Oven temperature: 350°F. 175°C. Gas mark 4.

Mix all ingredients well together. Using a teaspoon, place on a greased tray, well spaced out. Bake for 5 – 6 minutes.

Susan Hay, Camphill Blair Drummond.

Buttercrunch

6 ozs butter
8 ozs S.R. flour
4 ozs rolled oats

6 ozs demerara sugar
¼ tsp salt
2 Tbsps syrup

Oven temperature: 350°F. 175°C. Gas mark 4.

Rub butter in dry ingredients, then mix in the syrup to a firm dough. Break into pieces the size of a walnut, roll round with hands and place on a greased baking sheet, flattening slightly. Bake for 15 – 20 minutes.

Eva Hewertson, Kendal.

Hokey-Pokey Biscuits

4 ozs margarine
4 ozs sugar
1 dstsp syrup

1 dstsp milk
1 tsp bicarbonate of soda
6 ozs flour

Oven temperature: 310°F. 155°C. Gas mark 2.

Cream margarine and sugar until soft. Melt syrup and milk over a low heat, then add to mixture. Add bicarbonate of soda and beat until frothy, then fold in the flour. Shape into balls the size of marbles, flatten with a fork and bake for 20 minutes.

Eva Hewertson, Kendal.

Abernethy Biscuits

8 ozs flour
3½ ozs margarine
1½ ozs caster sugar

Pinch of salt
1½ Tbsps hot water

Oven temperature: 400°F. 205°C. Gas mark 6.

Sieve flour and rub in the margarine. Dissolve the sugar and salt in the water, then add to flour and mix well. Divide into small walnut sized pieces, shaping into a ball. Place on a floured board and flatten into a thin round. Prick well with a fork, then bake on a greased tin for 10 – 15 minutes. Cool on a wire tray.

Mairi Black, Rutherglen.

Shortbread

8 ozs butter
4 ozs caster sugar

1 egg yolk
1 lb plain flour

Oven temperature: 370°F. 190°C. Gas mark 5.

Blend, or cream together, the butter, sugar and egg. Gradually add the sifted flour, then knead to a soft dough. Cover a baking tray with greased paper. Shape dough with a mould and place on tray. Prick with fork and bake in the middle of oven for 40 minutes until light brown.

Muriel Gilray, Edinburgh.

Scourie Shortbread

8 ozs butter	8 ozs S.R. flour
4 ozs icing sugar	4 ozs cornflour

Oven temperature: 330°F. 165°C. Gas mark 3.

Place all ingredients in a bowl and knead together until you have a smooth dough. Place the shortbread into a greased Swiss roll tin and press down evenly. Prick surface with a fork and cut into even sized pieces. Bake for 30 minutes until golden brown.

Edith McDougall, Edinburgh and Mrs. E. Ormiston, Inverary.

Empire Biscuits

2 ozs icing sugar	Jam
8 ozs margarine	Icing
10 ozs S.R. flour	

Oven temperature: 370°F. 190°C. Gas mark 5.

Cream the sugar and margarine. Knead in the flour slowly, then roll out and cut into rounds. Place on a greased tray in the middle of oven and bake for 20 minutes. When cool, jam together and ice the tops.

Jean Simpson, Grangemouth.

Easter Biscuits

3 ozs plain flour	1½ ozs sugar
Pinch of salt	1 oz currants
½ egg	¼ oz peel
1½ ozs margarine	Egg white and sugar for tops

Oven temperature: 370°F. 190°C. Gas mark 5.

Sieve the flour and salt onto a plate and whisk the egg. Cream the margarine and sugar together, then add the fruit and ¾ of flour. Turn out on the table and knead in the other ¼ of flour. Roll out ¼ inch thick and cut into rounds with a 2½ inch cutter. Brush the tops with egg white, sprinkle on sugar and bake for 10 – 15 minutes. Cool on a wire tray.

Mairi Black, Rutherglen.

Cinnamon Butter Biscuits

6 ozs butter
4 ozs caster sugar
8 ozs plain flour

1 level tsp cinnamon
1 oz granulated sugar

Oven temperature: 370°F. 190°C. Gas mark 5.

Cream the butter and sugar until soft and fluffy. Blend in the flour and cinnamon, kneading lightly until smooth. Divide the dough into two then roll and shape into two 6 inch sausages. Roll each in granulated sugar, then wrap in foil to chill in the fridge. Cut each sausage into 16 slices and bake for about 25 minutes, or until edges of biscuits are light golden brown.

Lockhart McEwan, Rutherglen.

Alternatively, instead of using 8 ozs of plain flour, use 6 ozs of porridge oats and 2 ozs of flour.

Averill Marks, St. Andrews.

Custard Creams

6 ozs margarine
2 ozs icing sugar
6 ozs plain flour
2 ozs custard powder
1 level tsp bicarbonate of soda

For the filling:
1 oz margarine
2 ozs icing sugar
Vanilla essence

Oven temperature: 350°F. 175°C. Gas mark 4.

Pre-heat the oven and grease two baking trays. Cream the margarine and sugar, then add the sieved flour, custard powder and bicarbonate of soda.

Form mixture into small balls of walnut size and place on greased baking trays. Flatten slightly and ridge, using the back of a fork. Bake for about 15 minutes, then cool on a wire tray.

To make the filling, cream all ingredients together. Sandwich biscuits in pairs with the filling.

These biscuits freeze well in an airtight container.

Mairi Black, Rutherglen.

Tablet

3 ozs margarine   1 cup water
2 lbs sugar   1 large tin condensed milk

Melt the margarine, sugar and water together, and bring to the boil, stirring all the time. Add condensed milk, bring back to the boil and simmer for 30 minutes. Take off the heat, leave until it stops bubbling, then beat for 3 – 4 minutes. Pour into a greased tin to set.

Patricia Scott, Edinburgh, and Muriel Gilray, Edinburgh.

Fudge

2 ozs butter   4 Tbsps water
1 lb sugar   1 large tin condensed milk

Put sugar, butter and water into a large pan and stir gently until dissolved. Add condensed milk and bring to the boil. Simmer on a low heat until mixture thickens and browns; this should take about 30 minutes. Stir occasionally during simmering. Remove from the heat and beat well. Pour into a greased tray, and wait until it is set before cutting into squares.

Patricia Scott, Edinburgh.

Puff Candy

2 Tbsps Water   ½ tsp bicarbonate of soda
1 Tbsp syrup

Mix ingredients together in a pan and boil for 10 minutes.

Lockhart McEwan, Rutherglen.

Coconut Ice

1 lb granulated sugar	2 ozs butter
¼ pint milk	4 ozs coconut

Dissolve the sugar in milk, add the butter and boil for 8 minutes, testing after 6. When the mixture forms a soft ball remove from heat. Stir in coconut then pour into a greased tin to set.

Lockhart McEwan, Rutherglen.

Treacle Toffee

8 ozs soft brown sugar	2 ozs syrup
Water	2 ozs treacle
Pinch of cream of tartar	1 oz butter

Dissolve the sugar in the water, then add the other ingredients. Bring to the boil, then cook for 12 – 14 minutes, stirring occasionally. After 12 minutes start testing if ready, by dropping a little of the boiling syrup into a cup of cold water. If it becomes brittle the toffee can then be poured into a greased baking tin.

Lockhart McEwan, Rutherglen.

'Philly' Chocolate Drops

3 ozs Philly cheese	1 oz raisins
10 ozs icing sugar	1 oz chopped almonds
2 ozs glacé cherries, chopped	Chocolate vermicelli
1 oz stoned dates, chopped	

Cream cheese until smooth and then work in the icing sugar. Add fruit and nuts and mix well. Take teaspoons of the mixture, form into balls and toss in vermicelli. Put in small paper cases.

Mairi Black, Rutherglen.

CAMPHILL BLAIR DRUMMOND
FESTIVALS

For anyone living in a Camphill Community, festivals play a very special part in the life of the year. They are many-faceted jewels that sparkle and send their glow into the days and weeks around them. The inner warmth of Christmas, the pale light-filled green of Easter, the fiery yellow midsummer flames of St. John's time and the burning brown-gold of Michaelmas and harvest are all experienced and shared by each one of us. Be we cooks or gardeners, basket-workers or bakers, we are all a part of the great circle of the year and can feel gratitude to nature, to the animals and to our fellow-men, in each of whom lives the divine spark.

Sally Schad, Camphill Blair Drummond.

> The bread from corn, the corn from light,
> The light from the countenance of God;
> From the glory of God may the fruits of the earth
> Bring light into being within our hearts.
>
> Amen.

Martin Tittmann.

EASTER

Nettle Soup - *for silent supper on Maundy Thursday*

Nettles

onions

Oil or butter

Flour

Milk

Salt and Pepper

Nutmeg

Pick with rubber gloves the tops of very young nettles and wash them thoroughly. Fry some onions in oil or butter and make a roux with flour. Add nettles and boil with a little water. When cooked, liquidise and add milk or milk and water, with salt and pepper and a sprinkle of nutmeg to taste. This is a healthy and delicious soup, and you don't get stung at all!

Sally Schad, Camphill Blair Drummond.

Malted Milk Loaf - *for Easter Day*

Rich white bread dough

3 hard boiled eggs, dyed

Oven temperature: 430°F. 220°C. Gas mark 7.

Make an ordinary rich white bread dough, by adding an egg and using milk instead of water. Plait it into three after it has risen for the first time. After proving again and baking in a hot oven, scoop out 3 equidistant holes in which you place the eggs. The loaf is eaten at Easter morning breakfast, at a table decorated with fresh young leaves and eggshell vases with the first tiny flowers.

Sally Schad, Camphill Blair Drummond.

St Johns

Käseküchli - *cheese puffs or eclairs*

3 cups milk	4 ozs butter
pinch of salt	9 ozs flour
9 ozs cheese, grated	6 eggs

Oven temperature: 350°F. 175°C. Gas mark 4.

Boil the milk, salt, cheese and butter together, then add all the flour and beat well, until it comes away from the sides of the pan. Leave to cool slightly then add eggs, one at a time. Put teaspoonfuls well spaced out onto a greased tray. Cook for 20 – 30 minutes. Serve hot. Can also be deep fried.

Camphill Blair Drummond.

Agnete's Pudding

Juice of 4 lemons	2½ Tbsps cornflour
Juice of 2 oranges	4 – 5 eggs, separated
Finely grated rind of 2 lemons	Sugar
2 pints water	

Blend the cornflour with a little cold water. Heat the juice and water to boiling point, then stir in the cornflour. Pour into a wide bowl to cool then add the egg yolks, stirring well whilst doing so. Add sugar to taste. Whisk egg whites and add to mixture. Pour into bowls and cool in fridge.

Sally Schad, Camphill Blair Drummond.

Yogurt Pudding

1 carton natural yogurt	1 punnet of raspberries
1 carton fresh cream	Demerara sugar
3 ozs caster sugar	

Mix yogurt and fresh cream together, then add the sugar. Put the raspberries in a bowl and add mixture. Put in fridge until set. Sprinkle with sugar, then grill for 5 minutes.

Sally Schad, Camphill Blair Drummond.

MICHAELMAS

Michaelmas Vegetable Broth

After our harvest gathering the day before Michaelmas, the best and biggest vegetables are washed and taken triumphantly to the harvest table, whilst the rest go towards storage or the soup pot for our Michaelmas meal. Depending on how successful the season was, the soup will contain a mixture of potatoes, onions, carrots (if we have a year without carrot-fly), leeks, turnips, swedes, celery and a variety of herbs. Bread rolls from the bakery will accompany it.

Sally Schad, Camphill Blair Drummond.

Rødgrød med fløde *- fruit pudding with single cream*

Fruit	Cornflour or potato flour
Sugar	Single cream

The fruit may be mixed berries, or just strawberries and raspberries. Boil this with sugar to soften, then set with cornflour dissolved in cold water. Pour into a glass bowl and serve cold with single cream and a little white sugar on top.

Lisbeth Nielsen (Denmark), Camphill Blair Drummond.

Fruit Cordial

A wonderful Summer's sight is the kitchen table spread with bowls piled high with redcurrants, blackcurrants, raspberries and strawberries, all waiting to be processed, some into jam and jelly, some destined for the freezer and some for juice-making. This last is done by steaming berries, adding sugar and bottling the resulting concentrate. A warming drink can be made by adding an orange and spices such as cinnamon, nutmeg and cloves; lemon juice can also be added. This spicy cordial is very welcome at Winter parties – New Year's Eve, Shrove Tuesday and at Hallowe'en.

Sally Schad, Camphill Blair Drummond.

CHRISTMAS

100 Waffle Dough - *rich and delicious for Advent*

9 ozs melted butter
9 ozs sugar
6 eggs, separated
18 ozs plain flour

1 tsp baking powder
2 – 2½ pints milk, warmed
Grated rind of 2 lemons
¼ tsp vanilla essence

Whisk together the butter and sugar, then add the egg yolks. Mix flour and baking powder and add to mixture, followed by milk, whisking all the time. Whisk the egg whites and add to mixture, followed by lemon rind and vanilla essence. If using an electric waffle iron, cook mixture on 3½ setting.

Sally Schad, Camphill Blair Drummond.

Rødkål - *Stewed Red Cabbage*

3 lbs red cabbage
2 – 4 Tbsps butter
2 Tbsps sugar

1 Tbsp vinegar or ½ lemon
½ – 1 cup red currant juice

Remove the outer leaves then shred the cabbage. Melt the butter and sugar in an iron saucepan, add the cabbage and steam for a few minutes. Add a little water and vinegar. Cover and simmer until quite tender, 2 – 4 hours, stirring occasionally. When nearly done, add red currant juice and more sugar and vinegar to taste. Sliced apples are often added to give extra taste. This is a very nice vegetable dish, which is often served with roast goose on Christmas Eve.

Henrietta Nicolaisen, Denmark.

Brune Kartofler - *Christmas Sweet Brown Potatoes*

3 ozs sugar
1½ ozs butter

1½ lbs boiled potatoes
½ cup of water

Melt the sugar, add the butter and water. Mix well then add potatoes, gently covering them in the sugar mixture until they all have a nice brown colour. Serve immediately after frying. These potatoes are served with roast goose and stewed red cabbage, eaten in every Danish family on Christmas Eve.

Henrietta Nicolaisen, Denmark.

Christmas Bread

1 oz yeast
3 ozs sugar
3 lbs flour
3 eggs, beaten
½ tsp salt
¾ pint milk

8 ozs butter, shredded
8 ozs white fat, shredded
6 ozs currants
6 ozs raisins
4 ozs chopped almonds
4 ozs chopped lemon rind

Oven temperature: 350°F. 175°C. Gas mark 4.

Dissolve yeast in a little warm water, adding a tsp of sugar. When bubbling gently, add to the flour. Add eggs, salt and milk, then knead to a dough. Add butter and fat and continue kneading. Add currants, raisins, almonds and lemon rind. Cover bowl and leave to rise. Divide into 2 or 3 pieces and shape into long loaves. Leave to rise again and then bake on flat tins in the oven for 50 – 60 minutes. When baked, glaze with melted butter and dredge with caster sugar or icing sugar.

Sally Schad, Camphill Blair Drummond.

Tora's Christmas Biscuits

1 lb syrup
4 ozs brown sugar
5 ozs butter
4 ozs chopped almonds
3 ozs mixed peel
½ oz ground cloves

½ oz cinnamon
¼ oz ginger
¼ oz nutmeg
¼ pint rosewater
½ oz bicarbonate of soda
1½ lbs plain flour

Oven temperature: 430°F. 220°C. Gas mark 7.

Put all ingredients except bicarbonate of soda and flour in a heavy based saucepan, and bring to the boil. Then add bicarbonate of soda and stir well. Remove saucepan from the heat, cool slightly, then stir in flour. Work mixture with a spoon. Store in fridge for 2 days. Roll out very thinly and cut with pastry cutter. The dough must be kept cold. Bake for a few minutes in a hot oven.

Sally Schad, Camphill Blair Drummond.

Vanilla Kipferl - *little vanilla biscuits for Christmas*

6 ozs butter
6 ozs flour
3 ozs icing sugar

Vanilla essence or sugar
6 ozs almonds, blanched and
   ground

Oven temperature: 350°F. 175°C. Gas mark 4.

Mix all the ingredients together, adding the almonds last, lightly kneading them in. Leave the dough for an hour then roll out thinly. Leave to cool. Form little half moons about 2 inches in length and bake for about 20 minutes. After baking, roll quickly in melted, unsalted butter, and dredge with vanilla sugar.

Sally Schad, Camphill Blair Drummond.

German Cinnamon Christmas Stars - *makes 60*

7 – 8 egg whites
1¼ lbs icing sugar
Grated rind and juice of 1 lemon

½ – ¾ oz cinnamon
1 lb ground unpeeled almonds
Caster sugar

Oven temperature: 290°F. 145°C. Gas mark 1.

Beat egg whites until stiff, then add icing sugar, lemon rind and juice. Stir until thick. Leave aside a big cup of the mixture for icing. Stir in the cinnamon and ground almonds. Take small amounts and roll out on caster sugar. Using a star shaped cutter, cut out biscuits and put them on a baking tray lined with grease proof paper. Allow to dry for some time and cover with the icing that was put aside in the beginning. Bake at a low temperature until the icing turns light yellow.

Adelheid Stutz (Germany), Camphill Blair Drummond.

Blessing on the meal.

Weights and Measures

Imperial conversions:

1 pound (lb)   = 16 ounces (ozs)
1 pint   = 20 fluid ounces (fl ozs)

Metric Conversions:

1 ounce   = 28 grams
1 pound   = 453 grams = approximately ½ kilogram
1 fluid ounce = 28 millilitres
1 pint   = 568 millilitres = approximately ½ litre
1 inch   = 2.54 centimetres

Index

Salads, Vegetables and Vegetarian

Snacks and Savouries

Baking

Camphill Blair Drummond Festivals